When Prayers Are Not Answered

When Prayers Are Not Answered

Finding Peace When God Seems Silent

ELIZABETH ROCKWOOD

When Prayers Are Not Answered

Published by Hendrickson Publishers
P.O. Box 3473
Peabody, Massachusetts 01961-3473

Printed in the United States of America.

ISBN 1–56563–373–3

Third printing—April 2004

Cover design by Richmond & Williams, Nashville, Tenn.
Interior design by Pilcrow Book Services, Kirkland, Wash.
Edited by Judy Bodmer and Heather Stroobosscher

For my beloved husband, Bill,
and
for Floyd W. Thatcher, my first editor,
in heartfelt gratitude
for their generous gifts of encouragement
and belief in this book
from inception to fulfillment.

Praise be to . . . the God of all comfort,
who comforts us in all our troubles,
so that we can comfort
those in any trouble
with the comfort we ourselves
have received from God.
2 Corinthians 1: 3–4

Contents

Introduction

Several years ago, on a rainy winter evening, my husband, Bill, and I emerged from the warmth of a local restaurant. My impression was of the darkness, the chill wind, the wet puddles underfoot. A gloomy night, I thought, depressing—dreary.

A small boy stood with his father near the cafeteria door. Excited, he was pointing straight up into the sky. Following the direction of his stubby little finger, I looked up to see the storm clouds parting, revealing a lovely star twinkling brightly down on us.

The moment stays with me, stamped like a bright color photograph on my memory. The child's pointing reminds me again and again of the way we can swing our focus from our troubles and problems to God's ever present help.

Nevertheless, for all their beauty, we cannot touch the stars for they are far away. There are times, especially times of deep trouble, when this can seem true of God, as well. In such times, we wonder about his whereabouts, his purposes, and his relationship with us and those we love. As deep, core questions stir within us, we may find ourselves crying out with the psalmist, "O God . . . have you forgotten me?"

It was during such a time in my own life that I began looking for a book that would deal with my questions and help me meet them head-on. Not too thick, not too heavy—I wanted a book I could slip in my suitcase, carry to hospital waiting rooms, and keep on my bedside table. I needed one written in everyday language I could understand, a book that would speak to me warmly, simply, kindly, as one friend to another.

Although I could not find the book I was looking for, gradually answers began to come. They came through people in whom the gentle light of our Lord quietly shines, their answers born from personal experience. Some of them are living today. You may have heard of them, or know them. Some lived long ago.

Their insights, answers, and stories strengthened my faith. As time went by, I felt increasingly, almost irresistibly, drawn to pass on to others what they had given me. Bit by bit, the book I had never found began to take form.

Writing the pages which follow has felt like preparing for a gathering in my home. As each chapter unfolded, it was as if I were lighting the candles on our dining room table, turning on the porch light, opening the front door—welcoming treasured friends.

It is with a feeling of celebration, in its deepest sense, that I share with you these men and women who faced the core questions and brought me answers filled with blessing, comfort, and profound reassurance.

1
Where Is God?

Has God ever seemed far away? Did you ever feel your prayers were unanswered? Have you ever gone through a time of deep, even devastating, trouble and wondered if God had abandoned you?

Perhaps you have read "Descent into the Maelstrom," the famous story by Edgar Allan Poe. It tells of a fisherman whose little boat is blown by a hurricane into the path of a treacherous tidal whirlpool known as the Maelstrom. Caught in its current, the fisherman clings to his fragile craft, as he is swept with dizzying speed toward the whirlpool's swirling, downward spiral. Lonely is his struggle, as he battles to survive.

There are times when we, like the fisherman, feel flung by events into forsaken circumstances. Something we count on, such as an intensely important relationship, or the well-being of a loved one, or our health, or financial security is threatened or lost. Suddenly, as the psalmist expresses it so eloquently, we "come into the deep waters."

I remember one hot, summer afternoon several years ago, when a phone message threw me into a maelstrom. The medical report of a loved one was the opposite of everything I had hoped and prayed for. As I hung up the phone, I felt as if the earth were crumbling beneath my feet.

Esther de Waal once wrote, ". . . there can be no pretense in prayer," and there was none in mine as, gathering up purse and car keys to go to our loved one's home, I whispered, "Oh, Lord, have you gone off and left us?" A strange, desolate prayer for someone who had loved and followed Christ for nearly forty years. Or was it?

Passing through our house to the back door, I remembered, like a dimly sounding echo, our Savior's own words in a time of desolation, "My God . . . why have you forsaken me?" In my own world of cares, I identified. But, I was recalling his words out of context. Only later would the completeness of what he said from the cross come back to me in the form of comfort and guidance.

Just as I was opening my car door, our neighbor hailed me and crossed over from her yard into ours. She had heard our news.

"I'm sorry," she said simply.

Her kindness, so genuine, so straightforward, broke into my emotional whirlpool. A question suddenly surfaced, from the bewildered, hurting center of me. "In all this," I asked her, "where is God?"

I will never forget her standing beside me in our tree-shaded driveway and the quiet, steady answer spoken by someone who had been in the maelstrom herself time and time again: "He's there."

Suddenly, I felt the confused swirling inside me wind down to a stop like one of my grandchildren's spinning tops. Her words rang true and put me in touch with what I had known since childhood. Under the grief and anxiety I was feeling, "He's there."

Whether or not my prayers had been answered just as I hoped, still, he's there. Whether or not I had questions, still, he's there. Like the stars are there, though the night be filled with clouds. Like the sun is there, though the dawn has not yet broken. Like the earth is there, warm and strong under our feet.

Yes, but more than this, more than constant and steadfast, for the "thereness" of God is wondrously personal.

The lines of an old hymn express this well:

O Thou in all thy might so far,
In all they love so near;
Beyond the range of sun and star,
And yet beside us here.

There comes to mind a homespun comparison drawn from the memory of my husband's much-loved mother. Although she lived many miles away during the years we were coping with earning a living and raising our children, she had, nevertheless, "been there" for us in capital letters.

Just knowing she was at the other end of the phone was a comfort and an inspiration to do our best when times were hard. And just as she was committed to us, so were we to her.

Bill's mother was a person who lived close to our Lord. I see her thereness as being akin to the thereness of God. The Holy One is present for us, whatever is going on in our lives, inspiring and empowering us. As the old saying goes, "He's only a prayer away." He is committed to us and we to him.

In the minutes between when I received the phone message and my neighbor returned home, I began a journey from fear to faith, from turmoil to trust, from whirling down a maelstrom to steady ground—from "Where is God?" to "God is there."

Years ago, I drew some little note card designs depicting a bird perched on a sturdy rock in the water. Underneath, I printed those poignant words David's heart poured out in 2 Samuel, "The LORD is my rock." Both drawing and words expressed my own feelings as I put the card together. My neighbor, in the midst of our crisis, pointed me back toward my rock.

"He's there." A simple message, spoken in a driveway by one friend to another on a hot afternoon. Yet, through these words, our Lord touched me and drew me back to him.

The Holy One has a way of coming to us like that, in quiet, unpretentious ways. In a stable. As a carpenter. In the "still, small voice of calm" that cuts through earthquake, wind, and fire.

In the following months, I grew up in my faith. My capacity to trust in the love and goodness of God in times of profound distress, as well as in times of well-being, increased incrementally.

Gradually, it dawned on me that the path I had followed, in time of crisis, was an age-old path taken by countless thousands over the centuries before me. Biblical figures, saints, and contemporary Christian leaders had passed through the identical stages from devastation to feeling abandoned by God, through questions to renewed trust in him.

Perhaps you recognize these stages, like ancient signposts marking a road you also have traveled or may be traveling now. If so, take comfort in those who have gone before us. Be reassured as you come across their footprints. We are not singled out in our maelstrom times. We have company and it's supremely good.

The most outstanding tracks along this trail, the ones that count the most, were made by Jesus. His cry from the cross, "My God, . . . why have you forsaken me?" rings across the ages. Hauntingly, it is heard anew in every generation. He knows about the maelstrom. He has been along the path of devastation.

I remember reading a newspaper one day a couple of years ago and being struck by the comments of a local pastor, Max Lucado, in response to a tragedy. "The presence of pain doesn't suggest the absence of Jesus. He's no stranger to sorrow, pain, and violence."

Jesus walks ahead of us blazing the trail. It is something like our following a path at night through dark woods. Up ahead, criss-crossing through the trees, we see the beams of his flashlight showing us the way through. He guides us clearly, as he himself passes from questioning to his prayer of perfect trust: "Father, into your hands I commit my spirit."

Looking backward or forward across the ages, we can find fellow travelers on this path. Some seven hundred to a thousand years before Christ, the author of Psalm 13 sharpened his reed pen, dipped it in his sooty ink, and traced across his scroll the familiar stages. Feeling frustrated, overwhelmed and forsaken, he questions:

How long, O Lord, wilt thou quite forget me?
How long wilt thou hide thy face from me?
How long must I suffer anguish in my soul,
  grief in my heart, day and night . . .
Look now and answer me, O Lord my God.

But then, gradually, the psalmist comes home to faith and writes: "But for my part I trust in thy true love."

We can jump across the centuries to find C. S. Lewis leaving contemporary footprints along the same route. This outstanding scholar writes in his book *A Grief Observed* about his own spiritual journey following the death of his wife.

He passes the signposts, one by one, as he writes first of his desolation, the "jab of red-hot memory," the "tears," and the "pathos." Directing his gaze toward God, Lewis feels abandoned, as if there were a "door slammed . . . a sound of bolting and double bolting on the inside. . . . After that, silence."

When I read this book, I was startled to find this great apologist for the Christian faith, when struck by tragedy and loss, his prayers not answered as he hoped, asked precisely the same question I had asked my neighbor in my own crisis. "Meanwhile," Lewis writes, "where is God?"

But then he comes to renewed trust in the love and goodness of God. Facing forward in faith, he commits his unanswered questions to the Holy One, affirming, "I know the two great commandments and I'd better get on with them."

It is heartening to remember in the maelstrom times that many have passed along this well traveled road on their way to deeper faith.

To trust in the thereness of God, when the going gets rough is to find our balance, to discover firm footing and go on, instead of down.

"If you put your trust in the Lord He will send you strength from heaven," writes Thomas à Kempis in his timeless classic *The Imitation of Christ.*

Thomas Merton underscores the thereness of God with his beautiful prayer:

> I will trust you always though I may seem to be lost and in the shadow of death. I will not fear, for you are ever with me and will never leave me to face my perils alone.

It is my own prayer that, as the chapters ahead unfold, you will be strengthened in faith, as I have been, by the stories and words of real people like you and me whose witness highlights these pages. May they give you companionship along your way, answers to some of your toughest questions, and an ever increasing awareness of our Lord's never failing love and presence.

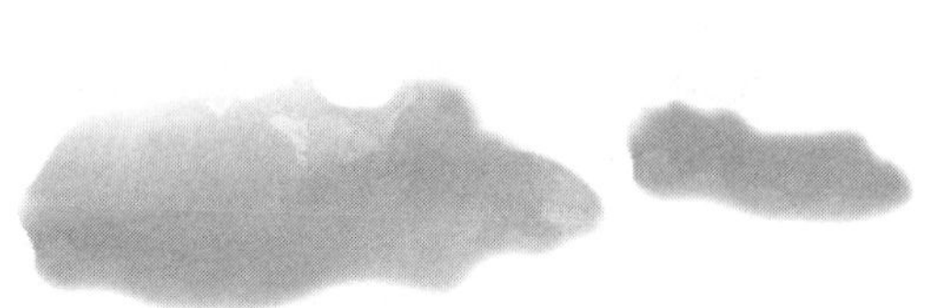

2
What About Those
Times When Prayers
Are Not Answered?

One winter, several years ago, I was visiting some much-loved friends for the weekend. The second night I was there, after the children were in bed, we settled down in the living room by a glowing fire.

As our conversation turned to prayer, I shared with them a true story I had recently read of a remarkable answer to prayer. They shared similar stories. Then my host suddenly said, "But still, I always wonder about those other times. What about those other times—those times when prayers aren't answered?"

How many of us, like my weekend host, have asked this question? If we haven't voiced it aloud, we may have wondered about it in our hearts.

Defining unanswered prayer as "denied petition for changed circumstances," Harry Emerson Fosdick writes that this experience can be "one of the sorest trials of our faith."

We pray about something that matters to us deeply. Yet, somehow, the answer we long and pray for never comes. In fact, as far as we can tell, there is no answer at all.

We feel abandoned. It's as if God had opened the car door, let us out by the side of the road, and driven off without explanation.

How can we understand this experience? Over the years, I have come to see God's response to our prayers as resembling a beautiful, intricately woven tapestry, such as I have seen hanging on castle walls in Europe and on the walls of the graceful Trinity University chapel here in San Antonio.

This tapestry of prayer I hold in my imagination is composed of many threads. There are the bright colored threads, and these represent answers to prayer which come, wonderfully, just as I asked for them. They shine and stand out in the fabric of my prayer life.

There are also strands of quieter, more subtle tones. These are the prayers whose answers come in different textures and shapes than I asked for, such as strength to deal with a problem, rather than removal of it. These threads, in their more muted colors, don't catch my eye as swiftly as the bright ones. I must look carefully to see them.

Last of all, there is another thread. Golden, shining, unchanging, it weaves through both bright and muted strands, touching with exquisite beauty the whole tapestry of prayer. This thread is the light of our Lord's presence, the gift of himself to me when I pray.

I pray and find myself touched by his hand. Something happens. I receive, however faintly, the imprint of his holiness.

I love the way Thomas Kelly describes this aspect of prayer. "We become new creatures," he writes, "making wholly new and astonishing responses to the entire outer setting of life . . . [We find ourselves responding] to life's demands in ways dimly suggestive of the Son of Man."

This golden thread of our Lord's giving of himself to us, this transforming contact with him, is so interwoven through the fabric of prayer that it can be glimpsed wherever and whenever people sincerely gather to pray.

One day, I stopped by a Roman Catholic church near our home. Although I am not a Catholic, I am grateful to this church for keeping their doors open and unlocked for those who need a quiet place to pray. This day, however, the church was not entirely quiet, as a service was in progress.

As I took a seat in the back, I was so struck by the priest's words that I quickly rummaged in my purse, fumbled my way past wallet, dark glasses, car keys, lists and sales slips, to my pen and hastily scribbled down his message on the back of an envelope.

Speaking quietly to his congregation, he said, "My good friends, what then is prayer? Prayer is the simplicity to allow our Lord to love us, to touch us—to change us."

In the sunlit morning stillness of the church, his words filled my being with this timeless truth.

Frederick Buechner, in his book *Wishful Thinking,* underscores this golden thread in the fabric of prayer as he encourages us to "Keep on beating the path to God's door [in prayer] because the God you call upon will finally come, and even if he does not bring you the answer you want, he will bring you himself."

It is meeting him that is at the heart of prayer, and as we draw close to him, those loved ones and concerns we bear with us are also brought into the circle of his light. We come to see this golden thread more and more clearly as we strengthen and deepen in our prayer lives.

When I was a child, an uncle came to visit. I was quick to check out what sort of gift he might have brought me. It was a picture of a horse I had asked him for and wanted very badly. All I can recall seeing of my uncle was the lower part of his overcoat, his shiny black shoes, and his two hands holding the picture. I have no memory of his face at all on that day.

But, when I grew up a bit, I no longer looked for gifts. I looked for the person. My eyes passed by the hands in search of the face, that I might meet and know and respond.

I think it is much like this with prayer. Petition denied can be the starting point, the cutting edge of growth for us into a larger, better faith. Yes, our requests matter. They are a part of the whole tapestry of prayer. But there comes a time when we see that encountering the Giver matters more.

Whenever a prayer of mine seems to receive no answer, it helps me to think of prayer as a tapestry—beautiful, whole, and made of many threads,especially the gold ones.

So much of our life is like this. We can't just look at a piece or a fragment and expect to comprehend the whole.

I am reminded of an experience I had not long ago. Last autumn, Bill and I decided to sell the house we had lived in for almost twenty years. We had moved there when our children were in grade school and had done the main part of our raising of them in this wonderful, fifty-year-old house with its sturdy rock walls and a yard shaded by a canopy of spreading oaks and elms.

But now our children, grown and married, had homes of their own. It seemed to Bill and me that the time had come to look for a smaller, easier-to-maintain place to live.

After looking around at available properties, we purchased a garden home. It was brand new and just the right size for us and our two much-loved Welsh corgi dogs. Fortunately, our old house sold at just about the same time.

After we had moved into our new home, I discovered I had left behind in the fireplace a pair of brass andirons which had belonged to my family for many years. The new owners had not yet moved in, so I went to retrieve them. When I pulled up in front of our old home, I noticed workers going in and out doing some painting and remodeling.

As I opened the back door, where I had entered countless hundreds of times in the past, a feeling I can best describe as love swept over me. The impact was strong, akin to the waves which used to bowl me over and toss me reeling at the seashore when I was a child. Startled and overwhelmed by the unexpected intensity of feeling, I stopped by the doorway. Tears welled up in my eyes and memories of our life in this house came flooding.

Hearing the workers approaching and embarrassed to meet strangers when I was so shaken, I hurried into the living room, gathered up our andirons, and left.

Driving home, I puzzled over what had happened. What had come over me? Was I sorry that we had moved? But Bill and I had wanted to sell the old house, and we were delighted with our new garden home. In every way, the new place was just right for us.

It was the memories, I thought. The memories of all the wonderful things that had happened in that house—all the wonderful things we had shared together in our home.

But as I reflected more, I realized all the things that had happened in our home had not been just as I might have wanted them to be. Instead, my memories were a composite of not only the wonderful things, but also the challenging, the difficult, and the traumatic.

There had been warm, loving days filled with the thudding feet of children, laughter, piano music, phones ringing, door bells chiming, and a barking beagle heralding the arrival of welcome friends of all ages.

Our son had gone to West Point from the old house and our girls to college and all three into marriages with spouses we cherish. More recently, the news of the births, one after another, of our wonderful grandsons had been celebrated in that dear home.

But there were hard times, too. There had been the deaths of Bill's mother, both my parents, my aunt and uncle, and one of our most treasured friends at far too young an age. We had even lost the old beagle and had buried his ashes in the back yard.

Tough financial times left us wondering how in the world we would ever get the children all raised and provided for. There had been some pretty hair-raising accidents and illnesses, and in 1989 our son had been sent as a Company Commander into the Panama invasion. We had known some sleepless nights and anxious times in that old, tree-shaded house.

But it was all these memories, both the wonderful ones and the traumatic ones, that struck me with such cumulative force when I walked into the kitchen.

The overall impact of these memories was of indescribable richness. My feelings were of gratitude for the life and the fullness of our years together. It was the whole of it, not just part of it, that had brought those tears to my eyes.

So it is with prayer. It is the whole of it, not just part of it, we need to look at, the answers of "yes" to our prayers but also the answers of "no" and of "wait" and answers that come in ways and forms we weren't expecting and answers which sometimes bless us beyond anything we ever knew to ask for. There is a fullness to prayer, its tapestry rich and varied, deep colored with wonder.

Yet, there are times when it is hard to see prayer as a tapestry. Sometimes, it is difficult to discern God's answers when our need is pressing, intense, and immediate while he, as the psalmist writes so poignantly, seems to "stand far off."

One of the best guidelines I know for tackling those tough times is to take a good look at how others have responded to this experience.

Just about everyone who has ever prayed can identify with the frustration of petition denied, from modern day Christians to the men and women of faith found in the earliest pages of Holy Scripture. Among this great host of companions are some who especially stand out. I think of them as Flashlight People. They show us the way and help us along with the problem of unanswered prayer. They remind me of an experience I had one night.

Our children were about twelve, eleven, and nine. I had taken them to visit my parents, who were vacationing for the summer in the Adirondack mountains in northeastern New York. During our visit, I happened to read a notice concerning a middle-of-the-night climb sponsored by a local group to see the sun rise from the top of a nearby mountain.

The participants were to bring flashlights and canteens and wear sturdy shoes. It struck me, foolish tenderfoot that I was, that this might be a grand adventure for the children and I eagerly signed us up.

The climb started about four in the morning. When we arrived at the gathering point, I noticed that not only were we surrounded in darkness at the mountain's base, but our trail, such as it was, led through a dense pine forest. I began to have uneasy feelings about bears and getting lost and about my wisdom in initiating this venture.

I also noticed there were no other children the ages of mine, nor any other early-middle-aged mothers. The participants appeared to be all of college age, fit, athletic, vigorous, and eager.

Daunted by the dark, the forest, and all the strapping youths, I positioned us at the end of the line.

As we made our way upwards through the woods, we straggled further and further behind the others. The path became increasingly faint and hard to follow. It was only the flashlight beams of those ahead of us, flickering reassuringly through the darkness, that kept us from getting lost.

After several hours of climbing, we neared the peak. Although the forest had thinned, the boulders we had to climb across were formidable and slippery. By then the four of us were all but shaking with fatigue and the pre-dawn cold. At this point some of the college students waited for us. I still remember the warm, confident grasp of their strong hands as they helped us over the worst of the rocks. Mentally, I dubbed my rescuers "the Flashlight People."

At last, we made it to the top, sleepily viewed a spectacular sunrise and then, weary but triumphant, clambered back down the mountain.

In just this way, I see the Flashlight People going before us along the path of unanswered prayer, clasping our hands, imparting their strength, and lifting us up and over the rocks.

Flashlight People are all around us. We can spot them, if we look. I think of a friend whose daughter was born deaf. She founded a learning and development center for the hearing impaired children in San Antonio, a response undergirded by her ongoing faith and prayers.

I think of a couple Bill and I are close to whose faith, prayers, and generous giving of time and talents to their church and community continue, despite their son's long, and finally lost, battle against kidney disease.

I think, especially, of one of our grown children's friends. This young woman's response to her husband's early death from cancer lights a path for any of us who have struggled, or are struggling, with the problem of petition denied.

Her husband had been a brilliant theologian and teacher, known and respected both in the United States and Europe. After the diagnosis of his illness, the prayers offered for his healing were worldwide.

Although he was not healed, she believed these prayers were answered, not precisely as asked, nor word for word, but on a deeper level. Trusting that "for everything there is a season," she felt certain that he had been given time to accomplish what God had sent him here to do.

She thought of prayer, not as a wish list, but as her response to Christ and as her way of answering his knock on the door of her heart. Through her husband's illness and following his death, she continued in her open hearted prayer relationship with our Lord.

Her ongoingness is in perfect harmony with the time honored response of the faithful through the ages to the problem of petition denied.

A little more than a thousand years before the birth of Jesus, the author of Psalm 22 expressed frustration with unanswered prayer. "I cry out . . . but you do not answer," he writes. Yet the rest of the psalm reveals he perseveres in prayer.

A modern-day rendition of this psalm by Leslie Brandt traces the psalmist's very real, intensely honest, unbroken prayer relationship with God:

> O God, why have You left me?
> Why are You so far from me?
> I can no longer feel You near.
> I reach desperately for You,
>   but I cannot find You . . .
>   I feel in this moment as if I am falling apart.
> Nothing seems to make sense anymore.

Brandt's rendition of the psalm continues reflectively:

I know, O God, that much of it
  is a matter of my foolish feelings.
The fact is, You are not far off.
You know both my feelings and my failings.
Yet You love me and accept me.
You will save me—even from myself.

Ongoing openness to God in prayer marks the lives of the faithful in holy scripture.

Moses' heartfelt petitions, both that God would send someone else to lead the Israelites and his prayer to see the promised land, were denied him. Yet he continued on in faith and prayer.

David's prayers for the life of his newborn baby were not granted. Yet expressing certainty that one day he would be reunited with his son, he continued on in faith and prayer.

Although Paul of Tarsus prayed for the removal of his thorn in the flesh, he never received the answer he wanted. Yet, he believed that our Lord was sustaining him in the midst of that trouble, and he continued on in faith and prayer.

There are many more such stories, but the crowning example of denied petition for changed circumstances takes place in the life of Jesus. Kneeling in the Garden of Gethsemane, greatly troubled as the crucifixion looms, he prays, "Let this cup pass from me." But the cup was not to pass. Yet he continued in faith and prayer.

There is a river running through these stories, both those from holy scripture and those from contemporary experience. This river sings with a river-like song, "Keep on trusting. Keep on trusting. Keep on trusting." The relationship goes on and the prayers go on no matter the rocks and turns along the way.

When I went to the Catholic church near our home in search of a place to pray, I was surprised to find they were having a service at 9:00 A.M. on a weekday. Moved by the peace of this place, its atmosphere of holiness, and the quiet devotion evident in those present, I went, thereafter, countless times.

One of the things that struck me was the way this service went on, every single morning, no matter what.

One time the air conditioning was out and in this hot Texas city the oppressive heat fell like a thick quilt over us. No one seemed to notice, and the celebration of the Mass went on as it always did.

Once the priest appeared to be ill with flu or a bad cold.

Sometimes noisy construction nearby nearly drowned the voice of the priest and the congregation's responses.

One morning a very old lady fainted. People sitting near her fanned her. The Emergency Medical Service came and revived her. But, all the while, the Mass went on.

I see this Mass as a parable for us when we grapple with the problem of unanswered prayer. The relationship with our Lord goes on, no matter what. The river flows on. Our prayers go on—a continuum from this life to the next.

A. J. Cronin, in his best loved novel *The Green Years,* writes of a young Scotsman's angry response to unanswered prayer. The young man, Shannon, is diligent in his studies, attends church, and prays repeatedly as he prepares to take a competitive exam for a university scholarship. Just prior to the exam, he is stricken with diphtheria.

Unable to compete and too poor to attend a university without a scholarship, he feels sure he has lost his only chance to further his education and fulfill his dream of entering the medical profession.

Regaining his health, he literally shakes his fist at the church of his childhood as he walks past. "So much for God," he says. "There is no God, no justice." Gradually the young man deals with and overcomes his career difficulties. In the novel's conclusion, Cronin writes movingly of Shannon's return to faith as, once more, he is walking past his church:

> Now, uncontrollably, he feels the need of communicating the exaltation of his spirit, in the listening stillness. He feels suddenly that his prayer . . . will not fall into the void. And with a shamefaced air, he darts into the dark church. . . . When he emerges . . . he sets off more briskly, his footsteps ringing clear in the empty street.

Cronin comes to grips with how intensely real the frustration of unanswered prayer can be. The river of Shannon's faith hit a great rock, was baffled, flung back, swirling and surging angrily. But then his faith moved past the rock, flowed forward, and continued on.

This ongoingness is the message of the Flashlight People. Centered in the Lord, we find them in books of fiction and in books of history, in the pages of holy scripture, and living next door to us. We pass them in the supermarket and see them at work. Their witness concerning petition denied can shoot straight and swift, into the mark of our own needs.

There is much to inspire and strengthen us, much to guide us, and much to help us send down deep roots of faith, should the winds of unanswered prayer blow strongly.

3

How Could A Loving God Let This Happen?

Several years ago, a dear friend of ours suddenly passed away. He had been having heart problems but everyone, including his family, thought his condition was under control. He had been a power for good in our church and community and was much loved. In vigorous middle age at the time of his death, he left behind his wife and young children.

In the months that followed, his widow kept asking how a just and loving God could have allowed this to happen.

One day, following lunch together, she posed the question once more, this time adding somewhat sheepishly, "How many times have I asked you this?" I thought a moment, then quietly said, "Probably about one hundred and forty-five times, give or take a few." We smiled; this longtime friend knew my response was lovingly meant. Nevertheless, the anguish behind her repeated question was not only intensely real, but a frustration shared across the centuries by countless others.

Again and again, as men and women experience undeserved suffering this troubling question arises. It has been grappled with in poetry, drama, and theology. Contemporary philosophy professor and author Peter Kreeft writes, "Like Job, I have wrestled with God about suffering."

It came home to me personally when our grandbaby had to go through weeks of radiation therapy. As I took my turn pushing his little stroller down the hospital's long, windowless corridors to the radiation waiting rooms, the question of a loving God's role in regard to suffering moved disturbingly around in the back of my thoughts. I wondered why he allowed the innocent to suffer affliction, not only for our baby's sake, but also for the other patients and their families around us, whose stories we learned and whose courageous efforts to cope touched our hearts.

Over the years, answers have come, bit by bit, like pieces in a puzzle falling into place. Gradually, there has formed a picture filled with meaning and reassurance.

I came across the first pieces for my puzzle many years ago, long before our grandbaby's birth, even before our children were born.

At the time, Bill and I were newly married, having breakfast in our first home, a little upstairs apartment in Texas City, Texas. It was a clear, bright morning. Our table was set with brand new wedding gift china. I had picked hibiscus blooms for a centerpiece. All of life seemed beautiful, until I opened the newspaper.

The headlines featured a grim account of a crime perpetrated on innocent victims. I couldn't even look at the pictures. I slid the front page across the table to Bill. "Why," I asked, "does God allow these terrible things to happen?"

My chemical engineer husband looked up from the sports section and then down at the headlines. He thoughtfully read the story through. "I wouldn't blame God for this," he said. "Just the opposite. If you get down inside this sorry tale, you'll find, not God, but a profound disregard for God and his will at its source."

I pulled the front page back across the table. As I read, I found unforgiveness, envy, hatred, and desire for revenge had fueled the incident. The reverse of God's will on every count.

For the first time, it came home to me just how much suffering can be traced, plainly and simply, to people turning away from God, the consequences spreading in waves of hurt over others. Waves that can roll through a family, pour out onto the streets, flow through a community, and engulf nations in the horror of war.

Here were my first pieces in the puzzle about suffering. As I fit them together, a picture began to take shape. The figure of a person was formed. His back was turned against a source of light and his shadow fell across a passerby.

As I think of this picture, I like to reverse it in my mind, reflect on what a difference it makes when people turn toward the light. We undoubtedly know many such people. It would be a heartening experience to quietly spend a morning listing them and remembering how each one touched our lives.

Everett Jones comes to mind, friend and mentor. An Episcopal bishop, he lived not far from us in San Antonio. He loved the tree-shaded streets near his home, and in his later years, he became fond of taking long walks. A dignified, white-haired old gentleman, he would put on his hat, take up his cane, and head out. In his free hand, he carried an empty sack. As he walked, he would pause, stoop, and pick up litter along the curbside. A Styrofoam cup, a crumpled soft drink can, a broken beer bottle—all went into his sack.

Whenever Everett Jones passed by, the neighborhood was a cleaner, more lovely place.

His whole life was like that. Everywhere he went was better for his having been by. The home struck by tragedy, the hospital room, the wedding celebration, or the board room. Strength, comfort, forgiveness, and hope followed in his wake. As in those graceful words that describe Jesus in the Book of Acts, he "went about doing good . . . for God was with him."

It is reassuring to remember there are countless people like Everett Jones, touching the lives of the innocent for blessing with more enduring power than those who touch lives for ill.

But, if much of this world's suffering hinges on whether people carry out the love of God or reject him, there still remain questions about undeserved suffering. The puzzle is incomplete, its picture unfinished.

What about suffering caused by nature itself—nature turned destructive? Viral infections? Faulty genes? Harmful bacteria? Disease-carrying mosquitoes? The droughts, floods, blights, and tornadoes which annually visit calamities on both humankind and the rest of creation?

On the one hand, we respond to the truth in the well-loved lines of Van Dyke's hymn:

Blooming meadow, flashing sea
Chanting bird and flowing fountain,
Call us to rejoice in thee.

On the other hand, another poet, Tennyson, writes just as truly of "Nature, red in tooth and claw."

When we meet nature in its destructive guise, our instinctive feeling is that something amiss needs correcting, like hearing a discordant note in a favorite song. At such times, we feel drawn, not to the rejoicing of Van Dyke's hymn but, rather, to help restore the missing harmony. We vaccinate against the epidemic, carry the sick child to the doctor, irrigate the drought stricken crops and battle the cancer.

In this response, we experience a profound sense of rightness, even of oneness with the powerful, redemptive drive toward healing and wholeness that marked the life of Jesus. In our small way, we join forces with the Holy One who brought peace to wind and waves, overcame disease, and triumphed over death. Yet, if Jesus' example represents God's will, why is there a destructive side to nature?

For a long time, I thought I would never find the missing pieces to this portion of the puzzle. The question seemed too broad, deep and complex. But one summer the missing parts fell into place.

One of our daughters and her husband became friends with a professor who taught at Austin Presbyterian Theological Seminary, about eighty miles up the road from us. Soon after getting to know him, they shared with me a collection of his lectures.

I was gripped by his writing, for he tapped into this very question. Pointing to a theme in scripture I had never noticed before, he developed the close-knit connection between human beings and the rest of the created order.

For the first time, I became aware that we not only share the most basic molecular structures with nature, but also, according to holy scripture, share a common destiny. I was really struck by this, for it explains why there are destructive aspects to nature, just as there are in human beings.

I began to read more on the subject and found a wonderfully concise summary in a Bible commentary: "Nature's destiny is inseparably linked to man's. Because man sinned, the rest of creation was corrupted with him."

From Genesis to Revelation, from one commentary to another, book after book and source after source, I found this connection between humankind and nature affirmed.

I began to see nature bound to human beings like a cart to a horse. The way we go, nature goes. In the words of the great poet John Donne, "As mankind, so is the world's whole frame."

As I reflected on nature's tie in with humankind, I began noticing how this plays out around us. For instance, just last week, Bill's and my eyes were burning. We puzzled about this. Later, from the news media, we learned that local ozone levels had soared. Respiratory problems and eye irritation were cited as harmful effects, pollution cited as the cause—clean air rendered hurtful by human beings—a discordant note struck in nature's song.

Understanding how this can happen in a close-to-home way helps me understand how humanity's historic, profound rejection of God and his will could affect nature on the kind of far reaching, epic scale described in holy scripture.

Here were more parts for my puzzle about God and human suffering. They were consistent with the first pieces and enlarged on them. As I fit them into place, my picture filled out a little more. There was the person, as before, his back to the source of light, his shadow falling on a passerby. As the new parts slipped in, his shadow extended further, touching grass, wildflowers, and a tree.

But if these pieces symbolize the negative side of humanity's connection with nature, it is comforting to know there is a positive side. An author of *The Interpreter's Bible* highlights this positive side: "[Just as nature] was involved for evil in man's fall, so she will be involved for good in his redemption."

We have wonderful glimpses of this redemption at work, even now. There are men and women all around us relating to nature's realm in terms of blessing. We needn't look far to find them.

This morning I passed a neighbor working in his yard. White-haired, sweating profusely in the hot Texas sun, he was down on his knees, staking up a young tree lest it blow over and die. Because of his care, it will fulfill its potential, grow tall, provide shelter for wildlife, and create beauty and shade.

Only a few blocks from our home, there is a veterinary clinic where we take our dogs, Nick and Mytton, and two pet rabbits. A sturdy rock building under a large spreading oak tree, this clinic is located at a busy crossroads. Beside the rush of swift, impersonal traffic, it stands as an island of compassion, caring, and healing. It is a place where humankind and the animal kingdom intersect for good.

Looking a little further, about a three hour drive from our home, there is a magnificent ranch born of a young man's love for nature. As a child, he had lived in the Texas Hill Country and had dreamed of sharing its rugged beauty with others. When he was grown, he and his wife purchased nineteen hundred acres along a beautiful river and established a retreat center and camping area for adults and children. Many of the facilities were offered free of charge.

Although this man and his wife are no longer living, their descendants carry on their dream. People continue to come, and nature—unspoiled, unpolluted, and carefully tended—continues to share the message he first heard as a child. This message is sensed in the sound and sunlight of the running river and in the smooth, various colored stones on the rugged hills, through the bird song soaring down the canyon at dawn, in the rising fragrance of sun-warmed cedar trees at noon, and in the cold clear diamond points of stars at night. More surely than a brilliant sermon, these quiet works of creation have drawn countless hearts closer to God.

But the relationship between human beings and nature, both for good and ill, still accounts for only part of the question about suffering. The picture in the puzzle is incomplete.

When our friend lost her husband and asked, "How could a loving God let this happen?" she was referring to God's power of intervention.

We cannot follow the path of faith for very long without stumbling onto the reality of miracles. They happened during Jesus' ministry among the men, women, and children in the towns and homes of Galilee. They happened in the lives of the early Christians. They happen today.

The revered former chaplain of the United States Senate Peter Marshall writes, "There are still miracles. . . . I have seen them. . . . There are clear evidences of God's power working in human affairs."

Perhaps you know someone who has narrowly escaped an accident or some other disaster, and you have heard them say of the experience, "Thank God—it was a miracle!" Their sense of deliverance was intensely real to them.

I remember a World War II veteran telling me of landing his plane after a mission on one of the small Pacific islands during the war. The mission had been long, he had gotten lost coming back, and the weather was terrible.

"The conditions were zero-zero," he said, "What no pilot wants, zero visibility and zero fuel. I had only one chance to come in. I either made it down or crashed in the sea." As he made his approach, unable to see where he was going, he suddenly heard the words, "Veer to the right." He did and brought his craft down on target, safe and sound.

But there was no control tower and no one to give him those instructions. "I guess the good Lord was saving me for some purpose of his," he said. "I've felt that way ever since."

Our Lord's interventions, his divine provision, can come to us in just about any aspect of our lives. There are times when God steps in and meets our needs in ways we can only describe as miraculous. We see his hand in these experiences as surely as we know his touch is on sea and stars.

I remember when Bill and I moved to San Antonio. Bill was fulfilling a lifelong dream, as he returned to the city of his birth and purchased his own business. However, we had not been here very long before the country went into a serious recession. Many businesses failed and went under. Bill went through an agonizing struggle to keep his alive. Burdened with concern for his family, employees, and investors, he worked grueling hours.

During this time, while the children were in school, I began making frequent trips to a little chapel not far from the house we were renting. This chapel was up on a hill in a lovely park owned by the Episcopal Diocese of West Texas. It was quiet, no one about and conducive to prayer.

But my prayer was neither long nor wordy. Drawn from the depths of my concern for Bill, I prayed, "Help him, Lord. Please help him." Day after day I went to the little chapel and prayed the same prayer. I told no one about these trips, not even Bill. They were between me and our Lord.

After awhile, a new friend, a retired corporate executive we had met in our church, joined Bill's company as a part-time consultant. His optimism, experience, and belief in Bill's company were a tremendous asset to Bill.

Some years later, after the business had come safely through those embattled times, I tried to express my gratitude to this man. His response made my heart skip a few beats.

"It's a funny thing," he said. After we moved here and joined the church, I prayed one morning—asked the Lord what he wanted me to do with all my free time. The answer came, just as plain and clear as I'm telling you right now—'Go help Bill Rockwood.'"

Someone once said the most amazing thing about miracles is that they happen. This retired executive was a miracle to me. He was an answered prayer wearing a coat and tie with years of corporate experience trailing behind him.

But if miracles happen, why don't they always happen? If God intervenes sometimes, why not all the time? Casting back through the pages of holy scripture, we find Peter miraculously delivered from death at the hands of Herod. Yet, later he was not spared martyrdom under the persecution of Nero.

My friend whose husband died was well aware that God's power can move in awesome ways. Yet God did not intervene at the time he so suddenly passed away. Why?

That was exactly the question she asked a family friend who came to visit her. He was a man of great faith, wisdom, and personal integrity. She felt sure that if anyone knew the answer to her question, it would be him.

His response was unexpected. "I wish I knew," he said. "That's one of the first things I'm going to ask our Lord when I get to heaven."

At this point, my friend let go of her question. It slipped through her fingers and dropped to the ground. She saw that the presence of mystery in the ways of God was, in itself, an answer. For the first time, she realized that mystery could be okay. With Job, she could say she had been dealing with things she "did not understand, things too wonderful . . . to know." And, like Job, she found peace in this humbling recognition and in the acceptance of mystery and the renewal of her faith in the midst of mystery.

Everett Jones once wrote, "There is a mystery about human suffering, especially about its distribution, that even the wisest and holiest of men cannot fully explain."

The existence of mystery in the area of God's relationship with human suffering should not surprise us, for mystery is a familiar part of our lives. It is all around us. We accept the fact of it daily and deal with it hourly.

How did our pet rabbit know to tenderly line her nest with fur before her babies came? What causes a man and woman to fall in love? Where do the stars end? How does our dog Nick know to go to the door to greet Bill before he could possibly hear Bill's car coming? Woven through the realities of our days are questions without answers. "The universe . . . is aflash with mystery," writes author-artist Helen Shoemaker.

Nevertheless, if there is a place in the pattern of our lives for mystery, there is also need for certainty.

In just about any area where I have to deal with an unknown, my first reaction is to look for what is known. For instance, if the balance in my checkbook doesn't agree with my bank balance, there is mystery. So I go back to certainty—my last correct balance—and proceed from there.

This way of coping with mystery is just as valid in our spiritual life. As we run into mystery, we can look for what is known. God gave us Jesus to be our certainty. The good Savior made no secret about himself. He is the city set on the hill of his parables, the lamp shining on the stand. All his teaching and all his life reveal to us One Who Loves.

It is enough information to build our lives on, to guide us, and carry us through the darkest times and the deepest mysteries.

Bill and I have a middle-aged friend who found this certainty during personal turmoil and unanswered questions. He had a demanding job. He also had a large family in San Antonio, which spanned four generations, and ranged from infants to senior citizens. Over a brief period, about three or four years, almost every one of these family members fell seriously ill from different, but long-term maladies. One by one, they became increasingly dependent on him. I will long remember his sharing with us how he coped with that stress-filled time.

"I got so worn down," he said, "I hardly had strength to go on. As I tried to meet my job requirements, while caring for their ongoing illnesses, theology and dogma became increasingly meaningless. Then, I began praying in the simplest way directly to Jesus, as to a friend. As I did this off and on through the days, there began coming to me stories from the life of Jesus, the man. I would think of him, as he walked the earth, the carpenter who loved children, a man who healed people and taught beautiful things about life, and who also experienced discouragement, failure, and suffering.

"And it came to mind that this man, Jesus, was faithful and trusting right to the end. And, as I thought of him so, day by day, I felt that he was alive and that he loved me.

"I quit asking, 'Why?' I just chose to love him and asked him to be love through me to others."

His story struck a responsive chord. I was reminded of a day during the long months of our grandbaby's illness. I remembered passing for what seemed the millionth time down those hospital corridors and silently praying, "Lord, I am yours. Even if I spend the rest of my life walking these corridors, I am still yours." Jesus was my certainty in a time rife with uncertainty. He was my strength and my focus. His message became simple and clear—we are loved by him and are to give love.

Through him, God is present with us in all the happenings of our lives. He is the answer to our deepest questions. With him, the puzzle comes together and the picture is complete. We see the person, as before, his back to the light, his shadow falling on a passerby, touching grass, some wildflowers, and a tree. The last piece fits into place to form the sun shining on a third figure, casting a nimbus of light about his head. He is reaching his hand to the other two figures, who are walking away.

I study the picture and try to imagine the two people turning around. As I think of what would happen should they turn and face this One Who Loves, words from Psalm 84 come to mind:

How enriched they are
who draw their power from You,
whose hearts are focused on You!
Even as they wend their way
through this fractured world,
they become springs of healing,
reservoirs of power,
to the sick, weak and empty lives
they touch about them.

4
Ways to
Come Close to God

How can we find God so he is personally real to us? How do we come close to him? How can we be sure of his nearness, especially in times of stress and trouble?

Years ago, I heard a World War II veteran respond to similar questions. We were in a small group together, during a church renewal weekend in Florida. Though I don't remember his name, I will long remember his face, his rugged features, and his story. He had been silent through the morning, taciturn and reserved. But when our discussion turned to the question, "When was God most real to you?" his reticence melted away.

"There was a time," he said. "I was eighteen. It was the morning of the sunrise invasion of Okinawa." He paused a moment, drawing on a memory still vivid after many years. "We were off shore," he continued, "on an aircraft carrier, just before the assault waves hit the beaches.

"Worship services were offered on deck. It was Easter, you see. Most of us went. We prayed together, maybe three or four thousand of us, maybe more. In all my life, God was most real to me then."

Suddenly tears sprung to his eyes. Looking down at the floor and shaking his head slowly, his voice hoarse with emotion, he said, "He was there."

I have often thought of this serviceman's story. His amazed awareness of the Divine Presence close to him in a time of deep trouble is an experience many share through the centuries all the way back to Mary Magdalene, as she turned in the garden to perceive the risen Lord through her tears.

How do people come to such certainty? The veteran's story gives a clue. During intense personal stress, when this young man didn't know if he would survive to see another day, he went where he felt our Lord was likely to be found.

Basically, if we want to come close to God, the best thing we can do is go looking for him. Pick up our feet and start walking in his direction; point ourselves Godward.

It is a two-way encounter. Our moves toward him are met by his moves toward us. "Man's face is turned to God through faith, and their eyes meet," wrote the Russian-born author Catherine Doherty. "God lives where we let him in," said an old rabbi. "Draw near to God and he will draw near to you," wrote the apostle James. If we are searching for him, we will eventually meet him. Many and varied will be the ways he reveals his presence.

C. S. Lewis writes of sensing God's closeness in the commonplace around him—a refreshing summer breeze and shafts of sunshine through the trees. "Godlight," he calls it, shining through ordinary things. "One's mind runs back up the sunbeam to the sun," he writes. "The sweet air whispers of the country from whence it blows."

Many have felt an awareness of the Divine Presence while listening to beautiful music. "I almost feel closer to God when I go to the symphony than when I go to church," a friend once told me.

I love the story of the little girl in Houston who said she meets our Lord in other people. "Oh, yes," she said, "I see him when they smile."

One of the ways God can make his presence known to us is through another person. We perceive him in their words, their actions, and in the quality of their lives. In them, we are met and touched by the living Lord. "He mediates Christ to me," a friend of ours said as he described a gentle, loving, God-centered member of our church.

Scientifically oriented people have been moved to a reverent sense of the Creator while exploring the unfolding mysteries of the universe. With the psalmist of long ago, they find, "The heavens declare the glory of God; The skies proclaim the work of his hands."

There are those who meet our Lord most intensely as they discover and fully express their God-given talents. Only recently, I listened to a tape of Puccini's flowing arias from his magnificent operas. I was moved by the astounding beauty of his artistic gift and thought of Puccini's memorable words describing his relationship with God: "When I am composing, I feel that he is close to me."

For some, the encounter with our Lord can be remarkably direct. I once went to a retreat in New Mexico led by Charles Whiston, an Episcopal priest who was then professor emeritus of Systematic Theology at the Church Divinity School of the Pacific in Berkeley. A Harvard graduate, an author, and the recipient of Lilly Endowment grants for research, this tall, reserved, accomplished man seemed an awesome figure. But, more than that, he seemed a holy person. Later, as I read one of his books, I was moved by his beautiful and deeply personal account of his call to the ministry:

> Can we remember times in our own past when we knew beyond all doubting that we were in the presence of the invisible God? I would share . . . one such time in my life. . . . I had spent two weeks camping in the Adirondack mountains of northern New York . . . [One night] about two o'clock, I found myself suddenly fully awake. . . . For some hours I walked or sat by the lake, the full moon lighting everything softly. I saw no vision, I heard no voice, but I knew beyond all doubt that an invisible presence which I knew to be God was confronting me. Without words I received the message from God: I was to resign my work with the cotton mills in Boston and . . . become a minister of Jesus Christ. There was no emotional excitement. I was as still within as nature was without.

Innumerable people can trace their own personal awareness of the near presence of God to that most beautiful of all books, the Bible. What the Swiss theologian Emil Brunner describes as the Divine-Human Encounter can take place when we open our hearts to the contents of these sacred pages.

In A.D. 386, a young man named Augustine picked up the New Testament epistle of Paul to the Romans and began reading at random. Augustine was a brilliant scholar and teacher. He was also restless, intellectually proud, dissipated and had rejected the Christian faith.

But on that summer's day, after reading but a few words, something happened. He had a mystical experience, an awareness of God powerful enough to change the course of his life. Describing this experience, he later wrote, "At the end of the sentence, by a light, as it were of serenity infused in my heart, all the darkness of doubt vanished away."

He was baptized, became a pastor, and later a bishop. He is remembered today as a major theologian of the early Western Church.

What happened to Augustine seems astonishing and inexplicable. Yet, it happened and happens still today. Our Lord meets us in scripture. Not just in times of great moment, but also in the little moments, the challenges, tears, and smiles of our everydayness.

We have a friend who was unable to sleep for worrying during his little daughter's long illness. As a result, aching fatigue made it more difficult for him to meet the needs of his sick child, his family, and his profession. So each night he turned to a psalm. He would get out his old King James Bible and go to bed repeating the last lines of Psalm 4, "I will both lay me down in peace, and sleep: for thou, LORD, only makest me dwell in safety."

Through these words there came to him a comfort and a sense of God's loving presence with him and his family. He was able to release his concerns and receive the rest he needed so badly for the demands of the coming day.

Holy scripture is like a special drawer in our bedside table, a collecting place for precious letters from a loving Father, messages alive with his caring, his guidance, and his encouragement.

I vividly remember a time—it was a maelstrom time—several years ago, when our Lord's nearness became intensely real to me through a single sentence from the New Testament. It was during our grandson's illness, a bleak and scary time for our family.

We had gone to New York City where he was spending long weeks undergoing treatment with a specialist. One Sunday morning, I woke up in the little apartment where we were staying near the hospital. I could hear the roar of traffic outside and see the tall, gray skyscrapers beyond the windows. Silhouetted against the pale dawn, these buildings seemed cold and impersonal.

I ached with concern for our grandbaby and his parents. I longed for them to be restored to the normal routines of ordinary living with friends, home, and the rest of our family. I missed these things as well. Although I had prayed constantly for our grandson and his parents, I now felt empty and drained, my inner resources beggared. I needed help myself.

So I prayed, silently, out of my emptiness, "Father, please give me something to hang on to—some words from your holy book to hold on to." As I lay there, a sentence from scripture came vividly to mind: "Fear not, little flock, for it is your Father's good pleasure to give you the kingdom."

I tried to recall where this came from. "The gospels," I thought. And then, "Jesus said it." But I could not remember the context and had not brought my Bible concordance with me to New York. While I was turning these words over in my mind, our grandbaby woke up.

My daughter and I spent the next few hours looking after him, preparing breakfast, and straightening the apartment. During this time, I kept reflecting back on the words that had come to mind, "Fear not, little flock, for it is your Father's good pleasure to give you the kingdom." I held on to these words. Although I did not understand why they had come to me, they seemed to offer a message of hope and a promise of better days to come.

Later in the morning, while my daughter looked after our grandson, I decided to go to church. I asked the doorman how to get to the nearest church of my denomination and he pointed down the street. There was one within walking distance.

I arrived in time for the beginning of the service and took a seat in the back. There were some hymns, prayers, and an Old Testament lesson. Then the minister got up and read the opening lines of the Gospel lesson.

His voice rang clear through the old stone church right to the back pew where I was sitting. "Fear not, little flock, for it is your Father's good pleasure to give you the kingdom."

As these words from the twelfth chapter of Luke's gospel rolled over me, I sat there feeling stunned, like a lightning rod that had just taken a hit. With Thomas Merton, I felt myself in "a world . . . charged with the presence and reality of God."

Like someone discovering gold and turning it round and round in her hands, I kept thinking, "He is with us. He is with us. He is with us."

Even if I could not understand why our grandbaby had to pass through this hard time and even though I had no answers to all the age-old questions about suffering, still I was certain the Holy One was with us in the midst of it. The strength and comfort of that assurance has never left me.

I more or less tumbled into this certainty, much the same as the young serviceman on the aircraft carrier came to his assurance. I just headed in a direction where I thought I might, somehow or other, come closer to our Lord. I turned to him in prayer, sought him in his word, and looked for him in church.

There are ways that can help us become aware of the nearness of God. Emil Brunner writes, "While God is coming to meet man he also makes possible man's going to meet him." These ways of drawing near to our Lord are simple, practical, and straightforward. Let me share with you three of them that have come to mean a great deal to me and to others I have known.

The *first* has to do with choice. Our choices daily, hourly, minute by minute directly affect whether we move toward God or away from him.

Choosing our Lord is something like choosing to face the sun. We can either turn our backs to it and look down at our shadows or we can turn toward it and be touched by its light.

Charles Whiston, while a student at Harvard University's School of Philosophy, attended a lecture which "proved you can't prove the existence of God." That same day, he happened to come across a biography of St. Francis of Assisi in a secondhand book store. Standing there, book in hand, he realized he must choose. "I chose Christ," he said.

Leaving the School of Philosophy, he entered the School of Theology. He subsequently became a powerful spiritual light to many as priest, seminary professor, author, and gifted retreat leader. Above all, he became a man of prayer, whose personal example inspired countless people, myself included. Choice was key to his ever-deepening relationship with our Lord.

Making choices which point us in a God direction will bring us close to him. We can count on it. I have a friend who suffered greatly from her divorce. The breakup of her marriage seemed to be the breakup of her very self. It appeared to her that all her dreams, hopes, and even her value as a person were hopelessly shattered forever in thousands of pieces.

It was a maelstrom time for her and she began spiraling downward on every level, physically, mentally, and emotionally until there came a time when she found little reason to go on living.

It was at this point that she started making a series of choices—God-choices. She looked for and found a church where she felt welcome and at home. She sought out women in the church whose faith was both evident and real. She spent time with these women. She asked questions, learned about daily prayer, devotional reading, and the strength and help to be found in holy scripture. She began incorporating this kind of prayer and reading into her daily routine.

One day, she chose to make a conscious, deliberate commitment of her life to Christ. Following this commitment, things began to change for her. She came to see herself as God's beloved child. She discovered the joy, power, and release of forgiving. A desire and a gift for helping others awoke in her. Acting on all this, she came into new and fulfilling friendships and experiences. The broken pieces of her life came together taking a new and beautiful form she had not dreamed possible.

One of our friends, Everett Jones, reflecting on the power of choice in his own life, wrote:

> At age twenty-one I left home and spent two years in New York City. It was a time of . . . learning who I was. The lesson I learned was that life is a series of choices. There I was in a strange land completely on my own . . . free to choose my own friends . . . my own forms of recreation . . . by what standards I would live. New York could be a place for beautiful and holy experiences or it could be a place in which to go to hell in a big way. I have found that all life is somewhat like this.

It was by his choices that Everett ultimately became one of the most loved and respected bishops in the history of the Episcopal diocese of West Texas.

There is a *second* way that can help us come close to our Lord. Time tested, it is as relevant today as it was two thousand years ago. This way involves doing just what the first disciples did: follow Jesus. Follow his example. Follow his guidelines for living. Above all, follow the message to love, which pulses through all his life and teaching.

I remember when I first became aware of the Savior's promise in John 14:23: "If anyone loves me, he will obey my teaching. My Father will love him, and we will come to him and make our home with him." As the warmth and intimacy of this promise broke through to me, I felt as our children must have felt when they were little and would flash like sunshine into whatever room I might be in, announcing, "Guess what, Mom!" This flash and this announcement always preceded good news—a new friend at school, a special invitation, a sports bulletin and even, with one of them, recognition of a new flower in the garden.

Reading our Lord's commitment to make his home with those who keep his word made me want to emulate our children's sunlight flashes and to carry the good news from room to room that everyone might know the wonder of it.

This promise of his is as real as gravity. During the winter of our grandson's illness, I came across a certain prayer. It was a call to obedience to Christ on the very deepest level. Written by the seventeenth century monk Brother Lawrence, it read, "Lord, make me according to thy heart."

My thoughts flew back to the time when it first dawned on me who Jesus really is. I touched again that moment of discovery when I realized that behind the conflicts, confusion, and contradictions of this life, there stands, always and forever, the One Who Loves. Reading Brother Lawrence's petition, I felt drawn to make it my own as well.

In the following days, his prayer began like yeast working its difference in me. I found myself shifting from centering on my fears and anxieties to centering instead on expressing God's love to those around me.

There was a wonderful sense of release and a feeling of rightness in this change of focus. It was like finding the highway you have been looking for on a bewildering, fast moving big city interchange. I felt the nearness of the Holy One, not in terms of some spectacular revelation, but in terms of this quiet sense of rightness.

The experience was akin to driving in a strange town with someone beside you who knows the way, someone whose directions cut through your confusion, whose knowledge of your destination eases your anxieties, and whose companionship comforts profoundly.

Nobel prize winner Albert Schweitzer saw the vital connection between obedience and a close relationship with our Lord. Firmly linking our experience with that of the first century disciples, Schweitzer writes that Jesus:

> comes to us . . . as of old, by the lakeside, He came to those men who knew Him not. He speaks to us the same word: 'Follow thou me!' . . . And to those who obey Him, whether they be wise or simple, He will reveal himself . . .

As we make an honest effort to follow our Lord's guidelines for living, he becomes more and more an integral part of our experience. Like a well loved family member, he takes his place in the center of our home. He is there when the guests leave and the shoes are off and the talk is from the heart. He is close to us in the morning times and the night times, in times of celebration and in times of sorrow.

A *third* way that can help us draw close to God is simply to put our trust in him. "My God; in him will I trust," said David. Yet it can be a challenge to trust the Invisible God when we are in deep distress, gripped by the icy hand of fear.

Trust in God can require from us the proverbial leap of faith. In the face of injustice, loss, and inexplicable suffering, it can sometimes seem all but impossible to have faith in a loving God. We may have to extend ourselves to trust him, to make a special effort, to dare, to risk—jump!

I am reminded of something Bill said when I was writing my first book, *A Wide Place for My Steps*. I kept coming up with reasons why I had no time to complete it. I had car pools, housework, community and church commitments, letters to write, sick friends to see about, yard work, and on and on. Finally, Bill said, "Just do it."

Trusting God is like that. We just do it. And, having done it, we find we are given new vision.

One of our grandsons, following eye surgery in Houston, asked with amazement how it was possible that so many tall buildings had been built overnight, along a familiar street. He was seeing for the first time what had been there all along.

Trust is like that surgery. It brings us into awareness of One who has been there all along.

To come close to God, we set our gear in a trust position. We trust that the loving God is with us, no matter what is going on, or has gone on, in our lives. We go forward in the spirit of Whittier's lovely old hymn:

> I know not what the future hath
>   of marvel or surprise,
> Assured alone that life and death
>   God's mercy underlies.

I have heard trust described as a "supernatural weapon that cuts our way through to the heavenly places." I was struck by the accuracy of the imagery.

Some years ago, our three children went to a popular local festival called Night in Old San Antonio. They were about thirteen, fifteen, and sixteen years old and looking forward to the food and drinks and craft booths, the games and folk music. But I was uneasy about them going.

My anxieties mounted as I thought of the immense crowds that flock to this downtown celebration. I recalled taking the children myself one year, and having, physically, to hold tightly to one another lest we be separated by the crush of exuberant revelers.

When they had been gone an hour or so, I turned on the television to get the evening news. One of those warning bands was beeping along the bottom of the screen issuing a severe storm advisory for the downtown area. Damaging winds, hail, heavy rains, and dangerous lightning were imminent. Viewers were cautioned not to go out in their cars and to stay home.

My earlier hazy, vague anxieties suddenly became full-blown fear. My imagination served up images of panic-stricken, trampling crowds, toppling power lines, and falling booths.

I realized that rushing to the festival was useless. I knew I needed to entrust our children to our Lord. But I also needed help to do it. So I got out an old prayer of Norman Vincent Peale's and sat down on the sofa and quietly prayed his words of total trust over and over:

> I place this day, my life, my loved ones . . . in the Lord's hands. There is no harm in the Lord's hands, only good. Whatever happens, whatever results, if we are in the Lord's hands it is the Lord's will and it is good.

Gradually, this prayer of trust "cut through to the heavenly places" and I felt the peace of the Holy One come into my heart. When the children returned home late, laughing and soaking wet, I was calm and ready to hear about what they considered a "really fun" evening.

I have used this prayer of trust, and others like it, often in times of distress, both large and small. I have turned to prayers of trust before scary medical tests, during a lawsuit in which our property was environmentally threatened, for areas of anxiety of every sort—even, most recently, during the problems involved in the illness of a beloved old family dog.

Trust in God is a winged thing. It soars over time and space, life and death. Bill's mother used the prayer of trust in the tough years following the loss of her eight-year-old daughter to polio meningitis. Many a time she prayed these words of faith from her well worn prayer book:

> Almighty God, we entrust all who are dear to us to thy never-failing care and love for this life and the life to come, knowing thou art doing for them better things than we can desire or pray for.

Thomas Merton, gifted author and scholar, writing of how trust puts us in contact with our Lord said, "By the gift of faith you touch God . . . his very substance and reality." That Bill's mother was in such contact relationship with the power and reality of the Holy One is best revealed by the way she never became embittered by the tragic loss of her only daughter. Rather, she was a blessing all her days to every living being whose path crossed hers—even to the wild birds she was feeding in her garden on the last morning of her life.

It has been said that trusting God in the dark times can be one of the greatest challenges of the Christian life. Yet the alternative is to abandon trust in him in the face of suffering. This alternative entails losing our greatest good and our greatest help. It is akin to closing ourselves off in a cramped room, doors shut, windows locked, and shades firmly drawn down.

Trusting him is a different experience altogether. As we put out trust in him, there is a sense of coming home and of entering the place where we belong—spacious, sunlit, with windows opening onto horizons which unfold forever.

Dag Hammarskjöld, skilled diplomat and former secretary general of the United Nations, vividly describes the effects on us of faith in God versus non-faith:

> God does not die on the day when we cease to believe in a personal deity, but we die on the day when our lives cease to be illumined by the steady radiance . . . of a wonder, the source of which is beyond all reason.

Trust, like oak trees, can take time to grow. If we are persistent in cultivating trust, it will increase in us bit by bit. "Trust begins to form in the center of who we are," wrote the gentle, whimsical nun Macrina Wiederkehr. Describing her own experience, she writes:

> . . . it seems as though the God who walks beside me remains so hidden and silent. Yet, slowly, as the seasons change, I move from doubting the presence of the Holy One in my life to a deep assurance that God, in Jesus, is comfortingly near.

We can also have this assurance. Our Lord gives us ways to come near to him. I am reminded of a footpath at a retreat center in the Texas Hill Country. I love to walk it. This path is formed of natural rock and concrete stepping stones and crosses a river bed. It runs along the base of a dam. As I follow it, the river spills over the dam, swirls in shallows around the stepping stones, and flows by downstream. The moving water reflects the sky's ever-changing light.

The ways for coming close to our Lord are like beautiful footpaths. The ways of choosing, following, and trusting in him form spiritual trails. We will meet him on these paths, we going to him and he coming to us.

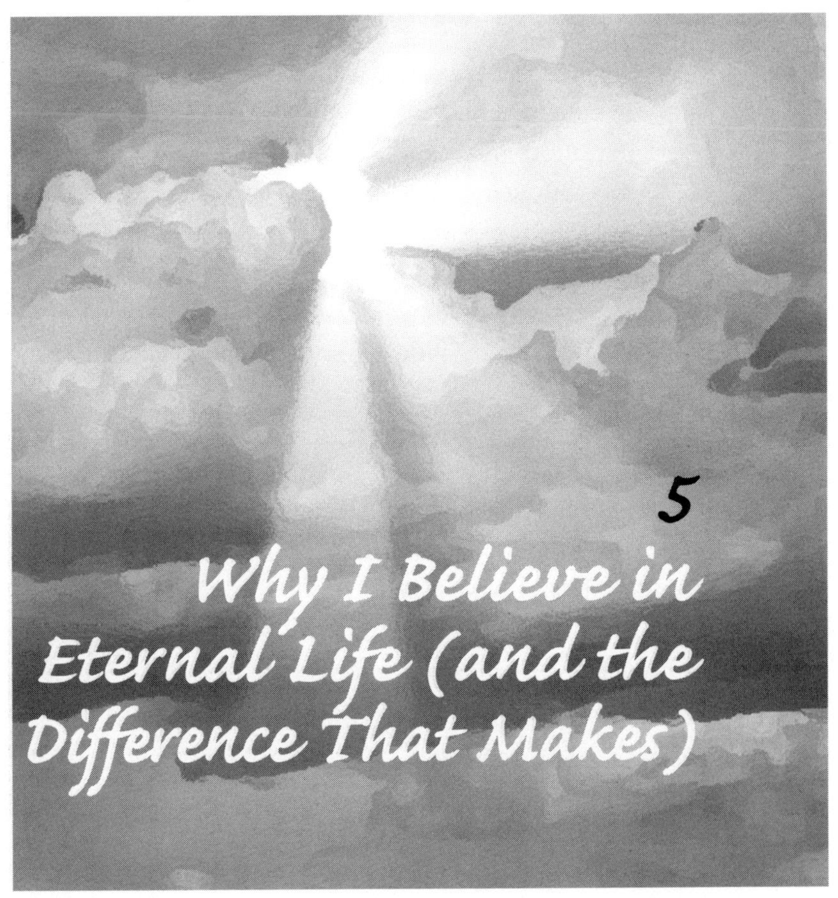

5

Why I Believe in Eternal Life (and the Difference That Makes)

One day I was showing one of our grandchildren a photograph of my mother. He had never met her, for she had passed away before he was born. "This is your great grandmother," I said.

The little five-year-old regarded her picture thoughtfully, then asked, "Where is she now?" How was I to answer him, this precious one, so small and full of trust?

Although scripture gives many assurances concerning eternal life, it is not a subject we talk about with ease. Most of us find it hard to envision a life outside this one we know, much less to put it into words.

When a friend of mine begins to comprehend something he will say, "I've got my hands around it now." But how do we get our hands around eternity? How can we bring into focus our Lord's promises concerning the life to come? Can we really believe his assurance and take him at his word? And if we do, will it make a difference in the compelling realities of life here and now?

There are answers to these questions, and our Lord has a wonderful way of helping us discover them. I remember a kind veterinarian saying to me once, as I brought to him our sick, dearly loved dog, "We'll work with you." He reflected the way of our Lord, for the Lord works with us. If we go to him, he will gradually bring us through our uncertainties to steadfast belief in his gift of everlasting life.

One of the most helpful insights that ever came to me concerning the life to come seemed to open up one day, like curtains drawn back from a window. I was reading the passage in John where Jesus, using imagery of shepherd and flock, says, "My sheep hear my voice, and I know them, and they follow me: and I give them eternal life."

As I read, the gift aspect of this promise struck me. I recalled his earlier words in the same gospel also referring to a gift: "For God so loved the world that he gave his one and only Son, that whoever believes in him shall not perish but have eternal life." Then I remembered that the apostle Paul spoke of a gift, writing to the Romans, "the gift of God is eternal life through Jesus Christ our Lord." It occurred to me that this aspect of gift is key to understanding the life to come.

One of the amazing things about gifts is that when people give them, they share a part of themselves. Large or small, generous or grudging, their gift is an expression of who they are.

This truth came home to me in a memorable way. I had been invited to speak at a church in the Rio Grande Valley. Because of heavy storms, air travel was grounded and the roads were flooded. I ended up taking a long, tedious bus trip to get there.

I happened to sit next to a man who told me he had come from a country deep in South America. He was on his way to visit relatives in Texas. Indian in appearance, age indeterminate, his inscrutable face was weathered and deeply lined. He wore battered sandals and rumpled, worn clothes. He had tied up his possessions in a string bag at his feet, except his stack of dog-eared comic books. He passed his time reading them.

I had brought along a lunch and about noon, I opened my paper bag and retrieved a couple of sandwiches and some cookies. Noting he had no lunch with him, I offered him half of mine. He seemed pleased and politely accepted.

Since I speak little Spanish and he spoke little English, there wasn't much conversation. After many hours, the bus stopped at my destination. Gathering up my things, I wished him a good trip, for he had a long way still to go. As I rose to leave, he stood. "Here," he said. "*Para usted.*" (For you.) Gravely, he pressed his collection of comic books into my hands.

I left the bus with mixed emotions. "He shouldn't have done that," I thought. "He was enjoying those books." I also felt a bit foolish, arriving to speak at an Episcopal Church carrying an armload of comic books. But, above all, I was touched by the way the gift expressed so much about the giver.

Our shared lunch had tapped hidden qualities in him. Appreciation and generosity had risen like sparkling waters from an underground spring. I was moved by his gift, for what it told me about the warm person behind the lined, weathered face.

I see our Lord's gifts in much the same way. They flow out of the depth and fullness of who he is. Consider his gift of peace. "My peace I give you," Jesus said, adding, "I do not give to you as the world gives." His gift is special, personal, and uniquely from him.

Some years ago, I walked from our home to a nearby athletic field. It was on a hill and I loved to walk there for the wind blew across it, rustling tall palm trees, and to the north

I could see for miles as the city stretched out toward the Hill Country. On this day, as I walked, I prayed for a good friend who had just been diagnosed with a potentially fatal cancer. A wonderful peace came into my heart. I felt certain God was with him and his family and at work in their lives.

The kind of peace our Lord gives is profoundly different from the kind the world gives, for the Lord's peace can come even in the midst of problems that will never be solved on this earth. Quietly his peace is given, softly it comes, spreading through us as sunrise sweeps the sky. We feel his peace, sense his presence, and know the Giver through his gift.

This helps me understand our Lord's gift of eternal life. Coming from him, it is part of him. He sends the invitations. His return address is on the envelope and the banquet is his design.

Because we can envision Jesus from the gospel accounts of his life, from the witness of the faithful through the ages, and from our own experience in relation to him, we can get a feel for the nature and quality of the life to come. Here is something we can "get our hands around"; something that takes the cold stone of eternity, melts it down, fires it to life, and warms it with the personhood of Jesus of Nazareth.

When Bill and I were expecting our first child, we found a picture of Jesus in a bookstore. After freshly painting the baby's room, setting up a brand new crib, and adding a rocking chair given us by my parents, we hung the picture. Now, more than thirty years later, although it is faded and chipped, I still treasure it.

In the picture, our Lord is seated in a garden. There are three children with him. The oldest, a girl, stands beside him; the middle, a boy, sits on the grass at his feet; the youngest, another girl, is on his lap.

As Bill and I hung the picture over the crib, we had no idea that our three children would come along—girl, boy, girl—just as in the picture. As they grew up, and even now, the picture helped me visualize them close to our Lord.

I think of the life to come as being much like the scene in my treasured picture. The haziness of eternal life takes shape and form in the figure of Jesus and the way he is relating to the children. The artist's rendition, so true to the gentle, loving Christ of the gospels, helps me envision the kind of life that will come from his hand.

To believe and accept our Lord's promises concerning the life to come changes our perspective in positive ways. It's like a house my parents rented one summer in New Hampshire. It was both pleasant and interesting. But to go outside was to discover its real worth. To see it, in its expanded setting, made a difference in the way you thought of it, treated it, and valued it. Set in the midst of a charming, old New England village, bordered by quiet streets that led to woods, meadows, a lake, and wonders out of sight, the house could only be really known in the fullness of its surroundings.

Our lives, like the house, are seen more truly, more completely, when viewed in the context of God's gift of eternal life. "We are citizens of a world which lasts forever," the pastor of a church I visited said recently. Such a perspective affects not only the way we look at our future, but what is happening around us every day.

Bill and I used to have a little place in the country which I loved. However, it was a long drive from San Antonio and we could only spend weekends there. For several years, we both worked enthusiastically improving it, pruning, digging stumps, and clearing rocks. We upgraded the water system and fencing and planted trees, shrubs, and flower beds.

But then Bill became involved with other commitments and was less and less able to go with me. Although I enjoyed going up there, I missed Bill and, after a while, it became clear that the 160 mile round trip drive and the work were more than I could handle on my own. Bill and I decided to put the property up for sale. Nevertheless, it was hard for me to part with it.

One day, while it was still on the market, I went up to tend to some young trees. As always, the pull of the place was magnetic. I loved it, from the little blue house with its pale yellow shutters, to the view of the hills, down to the sun-baked rocks in the grass.

But I was aware that these lovely acres were not mine, but God's. "The earth is the LORD's, and everything in it," writes the psalmist. I believed this, had believed it for a long time, and felt our property, and all that we had, were a tiny part of plans and purposes of his which sweep through this life right on to the next.

But, even with this belief, it was still hard to part with it. Quietly, as the sun passed in and out of the clouds, making shadows by the young trees, I turned to our Lord in prayer. "Lord," I asked, "you know I have loved this place, poured myself out working on it. Why did you put it in our hands and why are you taking it away?"

Simply, clearly, the answer came into my heart, "You are preparing it for someone else."

After the property sold, I met the new owners. I was struck by how it met their needs. It was the rainbow at the end of their journey and would be their retirement home. I felt I had, indeed, been preparing it for them, that it had been a privilege to do so and that the Holy One was now moving me on to new tasks.

Our Lord's assurance of eternal life rolls back the limits of time, expands our horizons, and absorbs us in intentions of his that go beyond anything we could imagine. It carries us toward the day when, as Revelation tells us, "He will wipe away every tear" and "There will be no more death or mourning or crying or pain, for the old order of things has passed away."

A young minister came to our church years ago. Fresh out of seminary, he was overflowing with the love of God. I will never forget one of the first sermons I heard him give. Stepping down from the dignified pulpit, he came into the middle of the aisle between the pews, took up his guitar, and sang his sermon.

After that memorable beginning, I noticed that joy was one of the hallmarks of his ministry. It was something he not only had within himself but continually imparted to others.

Yet before he entered seminary, he had known tragedy. His cherished little sister had died of an acute illness, devastating his family, and he had also experienced the loss of some close friends who were in an accident. He could have easily turned inward and fed on bitterness over those cruel blows. "It's a rotten world," he might have concluded, living out his days in cynicism.

How is it that he became, instead, a joyous giving person, a power for good, and loved by many? The answer can be found in his own words, spoken recently to a small gathering here in San Antonio. "There are some things that can't be fixed in this life," he said, "but God, in his time, will make all broken things new again."

I believe this, absolutely. We know it's true, even in the face of life's most grim, dark nights. There is a promise of morning down deep in our hearts.

I love to read the writings of a fascinating woman who lived in the fourteenth century. She has been described as the first great female author in the English language. Juliana of Norwich was a Benedictine nun, a mystic. She lived in times disrupted by social unrest and the terrors of the Black Plague. Yet her confidence in the love and goodness of God illumines her work. She is best know for a deep experience she had in prayer. At that time, our Lord spoke to her and said, "All shall be well and all shall be well and all manner of thing shall be well." And, when she wondered how this could be possible, his answer came: "What is impossible to you is not impossible to me."

If eternal life seems impossible to us, it is helpful to ask ourselves, "Has God ever done anything impossible or miraculous before?" There comes to mind his creation of the vast universe, of our own cloud-swathed planet, of tiny snowflakes, exquisite, perfect, not one of them the same.

Has God ever done anything astonishing in my life in a personal way? Bill and I have held each of our newborn babies, looked at one another, and whispered, "Miracle!" We could never have imagined, planned, or drawn up specifications for these three precious beings. God is doing the impossible all the time, all around us, day and night, in things large and small.

"Has God ever done anything miraculous in your life?" I asked a friend recently. She said, without hesitation, "Yes. Many times." Then she shared with me one of those times.

Not long after she was married, she and her husband realized his father was about to have a birthday. But he was not an easy person to shop for. He was one of those fortunate people who had just about everything he could ever need.

What do you give the man who has everything? Yet they thought he might be hurt if nothing were given. But then they realized it was Sunday. In those days, by custom and law, most stores were closed on Sundays in Texas. Further complicating matters, my friend's father-in-law was due to leave for an extended trip the next morning.

Her husband, one of the most gentle, Christ-centered men Bill and I have ever known, said, "Let's pray about it."

"We prayed," my friend told me, "but my mind stayed pretty much a blank. I couldn't think what to do." But her husband, looking up from his prayer, said that it had come to him that they should give his father a copy of Henry Drummond's book *The Greatest Thing in the World*. This little devotional classic would be the perfect gift—something of real value.

But, as they searched through the phone book, made calls, they were unable to find an open bookstore. "Maybe we have a copy of our own we could give him," her husband suggested. They searched their bookshelves through and through, but could not find the book. My friend's husband was deeply puzzled. "I felt so sure," he said, "so sure, as I prayed, that we should give him this book." But, clearly, this would not be possible and my friend went off to tend to household chores.

One of her tasks for the day was to go through a pile of mail that had accumulated on her desk. Among her unopened letters, bills and advertisements, she found a small package. She noted, from the return address, that it was from a recent house guest. Opening it, she found a fresh, new copy of *The Greatest Thing in the World* by Henry Drummond. There was a note enclosed from the house guest explaining that he had not inscribed the book, in case they might want to exchange it.

At a loss for words, she sat there for a while, holding an answered prayer in her hands. She took the book to her husband. Together, they inscribed it, wrapped it, and gave it to her father-in-law just before he set off on his trip. While he was gone, he read it and was deeply moved. He memorized the chapter from 1 Corinthians, on which the book is based, and was influenced by this great passage on Christian love for the remainder of his life.

Our Lord touches our lives in amazing ways. We need never hesitate to accept the concept of a beautiful life beyond this one on earth simply because it appears impossible to our finite minds.

If we accept his promise and put eternity in our pocket, we can carry it with us wherever we go. When we come into dark valleys, we need only reach down our hand to feel its reassurance.

I can think of no better example of this than the response of a husband and wife in our church following the loss of their grown son. There are many hard things to face in this life, but their experience must surely be among the hardest.

The young man lived on the east coast and had struggled with depression for many years. He was a gifted mathematician, loved music and books, and was family-oriented. But apparently there was some body chemistry amiss in him and, despite treatment, counseling, and medication, one day he took his life.

When the news reached his parents here in San Antonio, they went back east for the funeral, filled with grief that their long battle to help him overcome his depression had been lost. On the Sunday following their return the young man's father, who was an associate rector at our church, took his place in the pulpit, looked out over our congregation of several hundred communicants, and quietly spoke about his son's death.

We all ached for him and what he had been through. I will never forget what he said that morning. The words have come back to me again and again, in other times, in other situations, charged with comfort. After telling the congregation the circumstances of the tragedy and thanking those whose prayers and friendship had been with him and his wife, he said, "As for our son's future, I believe the God of love I know and serve will never forsake him, but will follow him through all eternity until he is healed."

Both he and his wife continued to be the warm, outreaching people they had always been. His wife shared his belief. It was not that she did not grieve. "We were devastated," she told me, some years later. But her grief was not the whole story. She had a deep trust that her son was safe in God's hands and that, one day, she and her husband would see him again. Her steady, loving manner, which has drawn so many people to her through the years, lends visible witness to her faith. Remembering her son, she said to me recently, "There is a peace about it. There is a peace."

When I think of this couple, I am reminded of the words of the Quaker author Thomas Kelly: "[Although] existing in time, [we are] rooted in the Eternal one."

How do people come to such profound trust in our Lord's promises concerning the life to come? With many, their belief springs from a spiritual homesickness. Contemporary novelist John Cheever, in his short story, "The Angel of the Bridge," traces the thoughts of one of his characters as he drives across a bridge:

> It was at the highest point in the arc of a bridge that I became aware suddenly of the . . . profoundness of my yearning for a more vivid, simple and peaceable world.

Going deeper, the gifted author Frederick Buechner writes,

> no matter how much the world shatters us to pieces, we carry inside us a vision of wholeness that we sense is our true home and that beckons to us.

More succinctly, the Old Testament author of Ecclesiastes put his finger on the mark as he wrote that God sets "eternity in the hearts of men."

Our uncertainties about the life to come can turn to certainties, as we spend time with our Lord. I am reminded of a friend who is in the railroad business. Concerned about accidents at crossings, he has been on a campaign to prevent them. Recently, he gave Bill a lapel pin. "I'm passing these out," he said, "as a reminder for people." The pin is formed like a crossing signal and reads, "Stop Look & Live." We could carry this advice into our spiritual lives. We can pause throughout our days, stop, look, take note of the One who said, "Because I live, you also will live."

My belief in our Lord's assurance of everlasting life came from stopping, becoming aware of him, and getting to know him. My relationship with him grew as friendship grows. I had my first glimpse of him through some special people in the church of my childhood. Their gentleness, kindness, and encouraging words drew me to him as from a blizzard to a warm hearth.

The more I came to know him, the more my trust increased. I discovered the profound rightness of his guidelines for living. And I found his power, so clearly set forth in holy scripture, is also operative in the lives of people around me today and even in my own life.

As I came to know him more fully, the boundaries, so tightly imposed on us by mortality, seemed to loosen, and slip away. I became aware that the presence of God with us is an eternal presence, greater than time, standing apart from time, entering into it, his power over it. The words of Psalm 90, paraphrased by Brandt, express this so exquisitely:

O God, You have always been God.
Long before the earth was formed,
  long after it ceases to exist,
You have been and You shall always be.

With You there is no beginning or end;
  time is not measured by decades or centuries . . .
O God, break into our short span of existence
  with Your eternal love and grace.

I became especially aware of God's relationship with time when he broke into my little span of existence with his love and grace, when our daughter experienced a miscarriage. It would have been her first baby and the first grandchild for both sets of grandparents. I had not been in close contact with a miscarriage before and had never realized how much grief is experienced at such a time.

As I left the hospital, I remembered there was a midweek communion service in our church that morning. I felt drawn to go to it. Held in a little side chapel, there were only three or four people present.

As the service progressed, the gospel for the day was read. It was from John 16. I wasn't paying much attention, lost in my concerns for our daughter and her husband in their disappointment.

But suddenly the words spoke right to me. "I tell you the truth," the minister read, "you will weep and mourn . . . you will grieve. . . . But your grief will turn to joy." Then the gospel message unfolded into a beautiful promise:

> "A woman giving birth has pain . . . but when her baby is born she forgets the anguish because of her joy that a child is born. . . . So with you: Now is your time of grief, but I will see you again and you will rejoice, and no one will take away your joy."

I looked up to a stained glass window directly across from me. Lit by the morning sun, it was of Mary holding her baby. As in a chemistry lab, when ingredients come together, fusing, and forming a substance, so did words and window come together within me. In that moment I knew that, although we had just lost a baby, there would be another, and the joy of it would be great. The moment was alive with this promise.

I knew full well that the gospel reading had significance far beyond my own little world of concerns. Nevertheless, the certainty of the promise remained. I went home and wrote the chapter, verse, and date of this assurance in the back of a little paperback New Testament I carry with me on trips.

Time passed and another baby was born. The joy of parents and grandparents was unbounded. Once again, I left the hospital, this time with an overflowing heart. But I had not forgotten my experience in the chapel. Returning home, I searched for the Bible in which I had recorded the promise. I wanted to look up the passage, read it again, and give thanks. I flipped to the place and was suddenly struck by the date I had written on the page, May 5, 1983. I got up, went to my calendar in the kitchen. This day, this wonderful day of the baby's birth was May 5, 1984.

There was a perfection of timing in the promise and in the birth that filled me with wonder and spoke to me deeply of God's power over life and time. Standing in the quiet kitchen, the little paperback New Testament in one hand and my calendar in the other, I was vividly aware that there is One outside of time whose hand is on our lives.

It is through close, intimate friendship with our Lord that we come to trust him in the sometimes joyful and sometimes painful realities of our days and in his promise of a life beyond this one. The author of one of the most beautiful and beloved of all the psalms writes, in his own personal way, of this very experience:

O LORD, you have searched me
and you know me.
You know when I sit and when I rise;
you perceive my thoughts from afar.
You discern my going out and my
lying down;
you are familiar with all my ways. . . .

Where can I go from your Spirit?
Where can I flee from your
presence?
If I go up to the heavens, you are there;
if I make my bed in the depths,
you are there.
If I rise on the wings of the dawn,
if I settle on the far side of the sea,
even there your hand will guide me. . . .

Search me, O God, and know my heart;
test me and know my anxious
thoughts.
See if there is any offensive way in me,
and lead me in the way everlasting.

6
Finding the Key to Answered Prayer

One spring morning I was preparing breakfast for an out-of-town friend who was visiting for the weekend. As I criss-crossed the kitchen from refrigerator to stove to breakfast table, our conversation ranged across many topics. After a while, turning to the subject of prayer, she said, "Did I ever tell you about a wonderful answer to prayer in my life?"

Since I had not heard her story, she went on to share it with me. I bring her experience to you now, for it touches on the heart and soul of answered prayer.

My friend had been a brilliant student. Graduate of a prestigious college and winner of a Fulbright scholarship, she went on to teach, write books, and become a respected leader in her community. Her brother, however, had been a poor student and had little personal success as an adult. Although our friend longed to have a warm relationship with him, his envy of her formed a wall between them.

Through the years, although she was continually affirming and loving toward him and his wife and children, he responded to her with ever-increasing resentment. She suffered bitter disappointment as her expressions of friendship were met with rejection.

Not knowing where else to turn, she began praying for her brother. She prayed often and earnestly that he would change. However, he did not change. But gradually, she changed. Her painful feelings about their relationship quietly dissolved, melted away, and were replaced by a deep peace and acceptance of him as he was. This peace amazed her, for it was something she knew she could never have achieved on her own. Moreover, her continuing efforts toward a good relationship with her brother had not gone unnoticed by his family, all of whom became warm, loving parts of her life.

On that spring morning in our kitchen, leaning against the counter, she reflected, "Yes, My prayer was answered. Even though I didn't receive what I asked for, I received much that I didn't know to ask for."

Her story highlights a deep truth. Prayer is opening the way for God to come into our life, into our joy, and into our suffering. The answers are what happens when he comes.

"Ask," Jesus promises us, "and it will be given you. . . . For everyone who asks receives. . . . " His words are clear and straightforward. The response to our prayers will be good gifts from the Father in Heaven.

There is a way to pray that can help us become aware of his answers and receptive to them. It has been used by Mary and Jesus and countless faithful after them. I think of it as "open-handed prayer."

This way of praying reminds me of the times when my children were small and I had to cross a busy street or hazardous parking lot with one of them in tow. Prior to crossing, I would reach down and take their little hand in mine. Many a time I would find it clenched tightly shut around some treasured object. I would have to coax them to entrust their treasure to me. Finally, they would summon faith in me and turn it over to the mysterious depths of my pocket or purse. Then, their fingers free to twine with mine, we would move forward to our destination.

Open-handed prayers are like this. We release our concerns to our Lord. Then, trusting him, desiring his will to be done, his purposes accomplished, we move forward in companionship with him. The answers to such prayers can be breath-taking.

One of the most memorable experiences I ever had with open-handed prayer took place when our oldest daughter was in high school. A dedicated piano student, she was working toward a career in music and possibly concert piano. As she progressed, it became clear that the upright piano we had given her was no longer adequate. The time had come for a better instrument if she were to continue developing her skills.

So she and I went shopping for a grand piano. It was a sobering experience. We visited showroom after showroom and I became increasingly downhearted for they were staggeringly expensive. After several days of looking, we found a beautiful secondhand Steinway. It seemed a real find. I went home and eagerly discussed its purchase with Bill. But after going through our budget, we realized the cost was far too much for us at that time. "It's out of the question," Bill said.

A few days later, I heard our daughter practicing a concerto. It was going beautifully when suddenly yet another string broke in her upright piano. The music stopped. Silence fell over the room where she had been practicing. It spread through kitchen and dining room to the living room where I was standing and right into my heart. Deeply I felt the wonder of her musical gift, her hours of disciplined practice, and the frustration she must be experiencing.

I stood by the window, looking out at the blowing trees, their shadows moving across the grass. I didn't know what to do. This was a turning point for our daughter. Choices of college, career, and the path she would follow in life lay immediately before her. A close friend had urged us to encourage her to put her music on the back burner, go to a liberal arts college, develop her other gifts, and broaden her experience. Might they now tell me this impasse with the piano was a blessing in disguise? But others, experienced in music, had told us her talent was God-given, and she should aim for a conservatory and focus on developing her gift to the fullest.

How should I pray for her? The late Scottish theologian Alan Lewis once wrote, "True prayer begins when we don't know how to pray." Standing in the stillness of our home, I realized that only our Lord in his infinite wisdom could know what was best for our daughter. My thoughts ran along the lines of the old poem:

Being perplexed, I say,
  Lord make it right!
Night is as day to Thee,
  Darkness is light.
I am afraid to touch
Things that involve so much;
  My trembling hand may shake,
  My skill-less hand may break:
  Thine can make no mistake.

Turning to open-handed prayer, I released the need for a better instrument to our Lord, asking that if he wanted our daughter to continue in a musical direction, he would help us and show us the way to provide it. I was open to his answer, whatever it might be. Above all, I wanted his will for her. Like the child crossing the street, I turned over what mattered to me. Then, fingers twined in his, I was ready to follow wherever he led.

That was on a Friday. Over the weekend, whenever anxious thoughts recurred, I would simply reaffirm to our Lord my love and trust in him. On Monday, we received a phone call from a cousin by marriage in Houston. A lovely, gracious lady of the old school and a deeply devout Christian, she knew nothing of our impasse with the piano, but had long known of our daughter's talent for music. She told us she had received an unexpected stock dividend and had felt moved by a strong desire to give it to our daughter. "Use it for her music," she said, "in any way you see fit." The amount of the dividend was exactly the cost of the secondhand Steinway. In all the years we had known my cousin, she had never given, nor had we ever remotely expected her to give, our daughter such a gift.

A few days later, an answered prayer rolled slowly up to our house within a large truck and was carried into our home by three hefty, perspiring moving men. The piano helped our daughter bring to fulfillment her gift for music in countless beautiful ways.

The late archbishop of Chicago Cardinal Bernardin wrote, "Through prayer I become more connected with the

Lord whom I serve." In open-handed prayer we connect with him whom we serve. We are like a dry leaf fallen into a running river. We move into the current of our Lord's will; we are carried along in the flow of his purposes. I never knew this to be more completely true than in the experience of a longtime friend of ours.

When we first moved to this city, he was chief executive officer of an investment banking firm in San Antonio. A dedicated Christian with a wonderful family, he was active in our community. However, he began to sense there was something missing in his relationship with our Lord. It occurred to him that the problem lay in his prayer life, which had been mainly limited to church on Sundays.

He started making time for prayer during the week. Every day on his way to work, he would stop in at a downtown church near his office. There, in the early morning quiet, he would pray for his loved ones, friends, and concerns. Throughout the rest of his day he would pause and silently pray. He came to experience the reality of the poetic lines:

> Lo, amid the press,
> The whirl, the hum, the pressure of my day,
> I feel Thy garment's sweep,
>   Thy seamless dress;
> And, close beside my work and weariness,
>   Discern Thy gracious form.

As time passed, he began to feel that our Lord had some plan, some purpose for him. It was then he turned to open-handed prayer, asking again and again that our Lord would show him what he was supposed to do.

And answers came. Step by step, day by day, a remarkable path unfolded. It began when he was deeply moved by a luncheon speaker, a physician, who told of his work in developing countries. Our friend went up to him afterwards and offered to help in any way he could.

A few weeks later, the hurricane of 1974 struck Honduras killing and injuring thousands of people. The physician called our friend with a list of needed relief items. Of high priority was the need for sixty-five hundred dollars for inoculating instruments to immunize the victims against typhoid.

The next day, our friend received a call from his rector that seemed touched with the light of miracles. "I hear you're rounding up things for Honduras," he said. "The church has been given a gift and the vestry voted to give 10 percent of it outside the parish. We have $6500 for you."

But that was only the beginning of his being swept along in the powerful flow of our Lord's purposes. Through a remarkable series of coincidences, he was able to borrow enough trucks to transport 40,000 pounds of donated food to New Orleans for shipment to Honduras and to garner enough donated seed to replace 75 percent of the ruined Honduran sorghum crop. Plus, he, who had never pictured himself in such a role, bumped along washed-out roads in the back of a van to help inoculate more than 10,000 people in rural Honduras.

Following his Honduran experience, he continued praying open-handed prayers. Daily he asked, "Use me, Lord."

Over time, he felt led to disengage from his business in San Antonio, work for the relief of suffering in Central America, and later serve for many years as an outstanding president of the University of the South in Tennessee. For those of us who know him, the fruitfulness of his life, and the channel for good he has been to countless people in countless ways, there can be no doubt that his open-handed prayers have been answered far beyond anything he could have ever known to ask for.

If answers to open-handed prayers can be on a mega-scale, as with our friend, they can also be intensely personal and deeply spiritual. In my growing up years, I had an experience which many people have had. I was often around an adult person who was perpetually critical of me. She belittled my youthful accomplishments, harped on my mistakes, pointed out my physical flaws with depressing accuracy, and unfailingly viewed my best intentions with suspicion. I was too young to note that her negative evaluations were fired at other targets besides myself and too inexperienced to understand that her condemnations were reflections of her own troubled self-esteem. Lacking this perspective, I was often and deeply hurt by my encounters with her.

Years after I was grown and had reached middle age, I could still feel the sting of her criticism. It seemed to me that what I needed to do was forgive her. Although I truly wanted to forgive her, and I tried to, I prayed to, the memory of that unhappy relationship hung cloud-like over the sunlight of my soul.

Finally, I turned to open-handed prayer. I gave our Lord my desire to forgive and my inability to do so, and I asked him to show me what I should do.

One morning, not long after that, an insight came, like an unexpected gift in the mailbox from a friend. With clear certainty, I saw that it was time to put aside my long struggle to forgive the person who had hurt me. Instead, I was to pray that God's light come over her like a blessing, pour through her, and fill whatever dark places there might be in her even as dawn replaces night. Somehow, at the same time, I felt sure that wherever she was, our Lord knew about her and cared for her.

I prayed this way for several weeks. One day, while praying, I realized I no longer felt any need to forgive her. The cloud had passed. Forgiveness had been more than accomplished. Like a once-valued childhood possession is put aside, as we move on to greater things, forgiveness had given way to something better. From that time on, I have been at peace about that long-ago relationship. The experience bears out for me what so many others know to be true. When we open our hand to our Lord in prayer, he will lead us in wonderful, healing ways with a wisdom beyond our own.

The key to experiencing prayers that will always be answered lies in our openness to those answers. It brings to mind one busy morning when I rushed through the breakfast dishes, fed the dogs, sorted laundry, wrapped an almost late birthday gift, and dashed with hurried steps from one task to another until, for some unknown reason, I stopped and stood very still in the quiet house. It was a sunny spring morning. The south breeze came softly through the open windows, whispering of new leaves, budding things, and blooming mountain laurel. It was then I noticed the birds singing—cardinals, mocking birds, and the gentle Mexican doves. Unnoticed by me, in the background of my busyness, they had been singing all along. Our Lord's answers to our prayers are like this—there for us, yet so often missed because of our preoccupations.

Some years ago, I received a phone call in the middle of the night from a lady in India. Between the unseasonable hour, which was later explained by the difference between her time and ours, and the fact that Bill and I don't know anyone in India, the call made a sharp impression and startled us. Afterwards, in bathrobes and slippers, we sleepily reviewed the event. The lady in India had read a chapter from my book, *A Wide Place for My Steps*, which had been reprinted and sent around the world by Norman Vincent Peale. She had a question about prayer, a question which so troubled her that she had gone to considerable effort to find my number and make her phone call. Why, she wanted to know, were her prayers not answered?

Subsequently, we wrote to one another, back and forth, and I discovered she had a veritable shopping list of things she wanted God to do for her. They were all family oriented. All worthwhile. But her hand was closed so tightly around what she wanted that it was difficult for her to receive God's answers.

One of the ways that can help us become more open to our Lord's answers is to form our prayer in three steps:

1. **Reveal**: We *reveal* our concerns to him.
2. **Release**: We *release* our concerns to him.
3. **Receive**:We *receive* and are open to the answers he gives.

I sometimes find it helpful to give visible expression to these open-handed prayers. As we reveal our concerns, we might hold our hands before us, palms up. As we release our concerns, we can raise our hands, palms up. As we express our willingness to receive his answers, we might bow our heads, place our hands before us, palms together in the classic attitude of reverence, trust, and acceptance.

Part of open-handed prayer includes letting go of our own timetable and accepting the Lord's. A few months ago, one of our little Welsh corgi dogs was sick from some indiscretions concerning things she found on the street. The veterinarian had prescribed a twenty-four-hour fast, followed by a meal of chicken and rice. Before the fast ended, this little dog looked up at me, wanting her breakfast. Her eager brown eyes and pointed ears clearly asked, why wasn't I giving her what she wanted and needed? I reached down, touched her head, and said, "I haven't forgotten you." Even at that moment, I was boiling chicken and rice on the stove so I could give it to her at the proper time. Suddenly, it occurred to me how much we are like my little corgi. We ask, "Why won't God give us what we need and want so much?" We can't understand it. It doesn't seem fair. Yet, he has not forgotten us. He's already preparing an answer for us and it will come to us in his good timing.

In open-handed prayer, we are constantly aware of the smallness of our vision and the greatness of his. Knowing this enables us to pray, as Jesus did, with a free, sweeping openness to his will. A few years ago, I was made acutely aware of what a blessing this openness can be. I had developed an abnormal heartbeat along with episodes of faintness and was scheduled for a diagnostic test. The morning of the test, I went to the church near our home where I often visit for quiet and prayer. I was anxious about what this test would entail and what it would reveal. Sitting in the cool stillness, a troubling memory surfaced. My grandfather died in our home when I was a child. As best I could recall, it was from such a heart as mine. It occurred to me then that I, too, might suddenly be separated from those I loved and all that was familiar to me. Anxieties closed around me like a tight, confining box.

My first impulse was to frantically pray to be well. I had known prayers for healing to have remarkable results in the lives of others and even in my own life. But, somehow, I knew it wasn't the right prayer for me at this time. I felt our Lord was drawing me to pray in another way. So I turned over to him everything that I was holding. I released the test, its results, my health, my future, and the length of my days on this earth. Then, with my hands open and free, our fingers met and I silently prayed, "Lord, I am yours. May it all work out in your own beautiful way—however that may be." As I prayed it was as though the perimeters of the tight box built around me by my fears splintered and fell away.

Walking down the steps of the church to my car, I was filled with an indescribable sense of freedom and joy. It was as if my spirit ran like a child before me turning cartwheels across the parking lot. There was joy, and beneath it—peace. I did not know, could not know, that the test and others would reveal my condition to be one which could be controlled with medication.

The gentle Cardinal Bernardin of Chicago, whose recent death caused such an outpouring of affection by the many thousands who loved him, had a similar experience in much greater depth. When he received the news that his pancreatic cancer was incurable and he had only a few months to live, he wrote:

> "From the very beginning of this illness, I placed my life totally in God's hands, confident of his abiding love for me. And because of this I have experienced the deepest inner peace I have ever known."

Although Cardinal Bernardin's circumstances and mine were greatly different, both our prayers were open-handed and both received answers that met our deep needs. We tapped into that wonderful old truth, so eloquently expressed by the

Apostle Paul, that nothing can "separate us from the love of God in Christ Jesus our Lord."

There is a graceful old church in downtown San Antonio of classic beauty. A stone marker outside commemorates Robert E. Lee as one of its founders. My father was an acolyte there when he was a boy. My husband was christened there. One of our daughters, her husband, and their sons are members there. Above the center aisle, near the high arch of its vaulted ceiling, there is a wooden cross with a lily—a symbol of the resurrection—carved in the center. I never look at that cross or think of it without being reminded that Christ overcame the worst this world can serve up, including death. Such an awareness crumbles the walls around our prayers and expands our horizons as we look for God's answers.

I was at a luncheon recently, sitting next to a friend in a crowded room. People passed back and forth and conversations rose and fell around us. For many years, she had been a bright light in our church, with her deep love for God, her commitment to serve others, and her sparkling humor. Now, as we talked together, she quietly told me of a time in her life that I had not been aware of. It was a dark time. Yet, through it, our Lord had been present, answering prayers she had never known to ask.

It happened a good many years ago, when the much-loved retired rector of our church passed away. This retired rector had been close to her son, who was, himself, pastor of a church in another city. A day or so before the funeral, her son returned to San Antonio for the service. Not long after he arrived, my friend's husband also died. Having her son with her at this time was an infinitely precious gift. She felt our Lord's provision in this timing, his loving care, and his answer to unspoken prayer.

"But that was not all," she said, as we sat together at the lunch table. In what seemed an island of quiet in the crowded room, she shared with me the rest of her story.

The retired rector of our church had also had a son, an only child, who was severely retarded. As his son grew up, our retired rector became one of the original supporters of a center here in San Antonio formed to aid the retarded. Before his death, our old rector had requested that any gifts given in his memory should go to this center. Prior to his death, my friend's husband also made the same request. Because both men were widely known and loved, the number of memorials turned out to be substantial. Moreover, they hit the center at a time when it was in severe financial need. The combined amount served to make a critical difference in the life of an organization both men had cared about.

Once more, my friend sensed God's hand in the circumstances of her husband's death and felt his presence reassuringly near her in the darkness of her loss.

Still there was more to her story. A day or so after the two funerals, when her son, friends, and relatives had gone and she was alone in her house, she had a surprising visitor. A small, beautiful dog arrived at her front door. Smiling up at her, as dogs do, he appeared to feel completely at home.

Refusing to leave, he cheerfully set about protecting the perimeter of her property as if he had always lived there. He had no identification and her efforts to locate his owner went in vain. In the days, then months, then years thereafter, the little dog was her constant, devoted companion. She named him Guardian Angel.

As my friend finished her story, her words struck a deep, responsive chord within me. I identified with her experience of finding our Lord present, personally and intimately, in the midst of pain.

When I think of answers to prayer, a picture forms in my mind of the days when Bill and I had our little place in the country. In the summers, I used to be fascinated by the contrast between the parched, sun-scorched landscape around us, its grass burned yellow, the leaves of native trees pale, drooping, wilting and the river we knew ran deep, down underground. We would tap our well, Bill and I, draw from this underground river, turning on hoses and sprinklers, releasing the cool, pure, life-giving water to the baked surface. In such a way, I see our Lord's love running river-like beneath the surface of our lives, flowing in healing, life-giving ways through our prayers. It is in our openness to him that our prayers are answered, those spoken and unspoken and even those we do not know to ask.

7
A Treasury of Prayers
That Will Always
Be Answered

There are time-tested prayers that can be of immense value to us, especially in times of deep distress. They are like treasures gathered in a deep chest. We can dip in, rummage around, and draw out the one that shines for us and expresses what we cannot find words to express. These prayers carry with them the assurance that others have used them and been blessed through them.

The prayers that follow comprise such a treasury. Many of them are the intensely personal prayers of people whose words and stories you will remember from the preceding chapters. They are prayers that were answered in the past, are being answered today, and can be answered for us in days to come. Like a door opening to a sunlit morning, they allow God's light into our lives.

A Prayer of Saint Francis

After you have prayed this prayer for several weeks or months, you may be surprised to find the words coming back to you as someone lets you know you have consoled them or brought them hope or been a source of joy for them in a time of sadness.

Lord, make me an instrument of your peace.
Where there is hatred, let me sow love.
Where there is injury, pardon,
Where there is doubt, faith,
Where there is despair, hope,
Where there is darkness, light,
and where there is sadness, joy.

O Divine Master, grant that I may
  not so much seek to be consoled,
  as to console;
To be understood, as to understand;
To be loved, as to love;
For it is in giving that we receive
It is in pardoning that we are pardoned;
And it is in dying that we are born to eternal life.
—St. Francis of Assisi (1182–1226)

The Lord's Prayer

One of the best ways to form prayer in harmony with God's will and purposes is through the Lord's Prayer. Many people pray it specifically. For instance, you might offer it with special intention for a friend or for a personal problem.

I once prayed the Lord's Prayer for someone who was at a turning point in her life. I would think of her as I was driving my car and pray for her, over and over, in this way:

Our Father in heaven,
hallowed be your name
[in my friend (and I named her)]
your kingdom come [in her],
your will be done [in her]
  on earth as it is in heaven.
Give [her] today [her] daily bread.
Forgive [her her] trespasses,
  as [she] forgives those who trespass against [her].
And lead [her] not into temptation,
but deliver [her] from evil.

As I drove and prayed, an insight came to me concerning her situation. I was astonished by it, for it was nothing I could ever, in all the world, have come up with on my own. I later shared it with her. She followed through on it and it led to the fulfillment of one of her dearest hopes and dreams.

The Jesus Prayer

This ancient prayer, also known as The Prayer of the Heart, is traditionally one to be repeated over and over. For instance, we can silently pray its simple words while walking, waiting in line, riding in an elevator, or doing some manual task. Its power lies in its two parts, the first affirming the historic, revealed truth of the gospels concerning Christ, the second part expressing the truth about ourselves, which is our profound need of him.

In use by early Christian monks, by countless men and women through the centuries and into contemporary times, Swedish author, Per-Olof Sjögren, writes of the way this prayer affects him personally today:

> I come home tired after a long day's work . . . weary and aching from grappling with all the questions and problems of the day. Everything in me is crying out for rest. . . . The Jesus Prayer can move me from nervous exhaustion to composure and peace. It is easy to pray . . . it sets hallowed, meaningful words on my lips and in my heart, and it puts me at once in touch with my Lord.

Here is the prayer prayed by Christians for nearly two thousand years:

Lord Jesus Christ, Son of God, have mercy on me.

Five Short, Powerful Prayers

Brother Lawrence was remembered by those who knew him personally as "one who walked with Christ . . . one who saw God's glory shining in the commonplace." His few "conversations" and brief letters have been read again and again by literally millions of people across three centuries. He prayed: "Lord, make me according to your heart."

Several years ago, Bill and I were privileged to hear a visiting pastor from London here in San Antonio. A man of deep faith and the rector of a large parish, he was wonderfully gifted and articulate. What struck me most was the prayer with which he starts his day. Offering all that he is and all that he has to our Lord and to the service of others, he prays: "For thee. For them. Amen."

Norman Vincent Peale was a blessing to many during his lifetime with his emphasis on a positive, upbeat approach to life. He was never more so than with a prayer he recommended to a woman who felt defeated by her many troubles. He advised her to prayerfully repeat a simple, threefold statement of faith on awakening in the morning—one which would, and did, make a powerful difference in the way her life played out. The words were: "I believe. I believe. I believe."

There is an oft-used prayer I love. It is a wonderful one to use while driving to work, before a family gathering, at a party or just about any time: "Dear Lord, Please use me to bless someone. In Jesus' name. Amen."

Bill's and my friend, who was instrumental in the relief of Honduran hurricane victims and whose life was subsequently so remarkably fruitful, has a prayer which is special to him. He describes it as "the key to a happy and worthwhile life." Here is his prayer: "Use me today, Lord."

Asking How to Pray

"Lord, teach us to pray," said the first disciples. We are in good company when we ask God's help with our prayers. Even Jesus, in a time of personal crisis, began his prayer, "Now is my heart troubled, and what shall I say?"

Many people ask our Lord how they should pray. If we persist, his guidance comes. We pass from uncertainty to certainty. A prayer comes into focus which is in harmony with his will. I remember when my mother was terminally ill and seemed to feel her course was run, her life completed. I didn't know how to form my prayers. As I asked, "How shall I pray, Lord?" it came clearly that I should pray for her highest good in his sight. With this prayer came a deep sense of peace.

Cries for Help

Cries for help can be short and to the point. Brother Lawrence, carrying out his duties as monastery cook, often felt his assigned tasks were beyond his abilities. He would pray: "Lord, I cannot do this unless you help me." Our Lord, he reported, never failed to help him.

When a friend of mine and Bill's was faced with the massive relief needs of the Honduran hurricane victims, he said, "I dropped my head and prayed as earnestly as I could, 'Help me, Lord.'"

Our cries for help have been called "foxhole prayers" and "arrow prayers," for they are shot, almost without thought, to One greater than ourselves in time of need. They can be as short as one word, as we open our hearts and whisper, "Jesus."

A Simple, Beautiful Way to Pray

In this way of prayer, we simply sit quietly, resting our arms on our lap with our hands open and palms up. Then we bring before our Lord the person or situation we are concerned about, saying, "Lord, I bring you this person" or "Lord, here is this trouble." Naming the person or identifying the trouble, we quietly hold this concern in his light for a while. It is a wonderful way to pray.

An Imaging Prayer

Similar to the preceding prayer is imaging prayer. In this kind of prayer, we become still and form a picture in our minds of our Lord Jesus Christ. Then we picture the person we are concerned about coming into his presence, into the circle of life, love, and holiness that surrounds him. If it is a child, we might picture ourselves placing this child on his lap. If it is an adult, we might picture ourselves holding his or her hand or standing near the person. We quietly hold this picture for awhile and then give thanks to our Lord and bless his name.

Course-Correction Prayers

Sometimes when we pray, we are like an airline pilot flying through fog. We need to contact the control tower and find out if we need a course correction. As a pilot opens himself to making necessary changes, so do we in our course-correction prayers. Such prayers are answered, as those of us who have prayed them can attest. There is no better example of this kind of prayer than Leslie Brandt's paraphrase of David's psalm:

> May your all-knowing, everywhere-present Spirit
> continue to search out my feelings and thoughts.
> Deliver me
> from that which may hurt or destroy me,
> and guide me along the paths of love and truth.

Giving Thanks

Jesus underlined the importance of a thankful heart, giving thanks himself and affirming those who were thankful. To pray in thanksgiving for obvious gifts opens us to God, brings us into right relationship with him, and reminds us that our very life is his gift. Giving thanks for the less obvious is more challenging.

Some years ago, I attended a retreat led by a bishop from England. Referring to the Apostle Paul's counsel that we be "always giving thanks to God the Father for everything," he recommended that we give thanks for the difficult people in our lives, just as they are. Such prayers, he said, express our faith and trust in God and open the way for surprising answers.

During the closing service of the retreat, I began praying in this way for a person who had broken off communications with our family in a fit of anger. At first, I found it hard to do, but I kept at it. A few weeks later, after I had been daily giving thanks for her, she sent us a toaster oven through the mail, along with a card simply saying she hoped we would enjoy it. That she had suddenly broken her longtime silence in such a surprising way was astonishing. The next morning, sliding sizzling biscuits from the shiny, new oven, it seemed a little miracle to me, a gentle token that prayer had been used to warm a frozen relationship.

Prayers of thanksgiving, in such situations, are born of sheer faith that the redemptive love of God is at work despite outward appearances. To put this prayer in words, we might pray simply: "Dear Father in Heaven, I don't understand [name of person] but, in trust, I give thanks for her [him] just as she [he] is. In Jesus' name, Amen."

Prayers of Adoration

We open ourselves to our Lord's answers in a special way through prayers of adoration. I remember as a child in summer camp in Maine being filled with silent adoration for God through the exquisite beauty of his creation. In response he filled my heart with a love for him that has lasted all my life.

He answers our prayers of adoration, silent or spoken, in his own way. Bill and I had a friend, now deceased, who expressed his adoration by often praying the opening words of Psalm 103: "Bless the LORD, O my soul: and all that is within me, bless his holy name." Our Lord's answer to his oft-repeated prayer guided our friend's life so that he became a blessing to countless others.

Praying from the Bible

The holy scriptures offer powerful guidelines for our prayers and can help us become open to our Lord and his answers. For instance, if we are concerned about someone who has no faith, we might align our prayer with the Apostle Paul's prayer in Romans 15: "Father, May [name of person] be filled 'with all joy and peace in believing.'" Or, if our own faith is shaky, we might pray from Mark's gospel: "I believe, help thou my unbelief."

Should we find ourselves in truly desperate circumstances, perhaps even sensing that we may be approaching the end of our earthly journey, we can be assured that our Lord has been there before us, giving us his own words to guide our prayer: "Father, into your hands I commit my spirit."

Prayers for Specific Concerns

For a Child

Dear Lord,
Thank you for your gift of this child in our lives. Please may one of your dear angels watch over this little one all of his [her] days and bring this child to the fulfillment of your perfect will for him [her].

In Jesus' name,
Amen

For Grown Children

They are grown now, Lord, my hands are emptied
Of the countless tasks required for so long,
And I am helpless quite before the problems
That grown children face. I cannot right Earth's wrongs,
Or smooth their pathways, but, dear Lord, You can.
Speak to them face to face, as person to person.

I have no legacy at all to give them,
But if my prayer be answered, it will give
Them more than any wealth the world can offer.
I pray: Christ be their comrade while they live.
Walk with them should they feel they walk alone,
And make Your presence, daily, hourly known.

Companion them. I ask for nothing greater
Than this rich blessing for these precious ones:
The holy companionship of Christ
As counselor and guide to these, my children.
I loose their hands, having done all I could do,
And trust them, Lord, implicitly to You.

Grace Noll Crowell
(Adapted)

For Loved Ones

Almighty God,
We entrust all who are dear to us
to your never-failing care and love
for this life and the life to come,
knowing you are doing for them better things
than we can desire or pray for
through Jesus Christ, our Lord.

Amen.

—*The Book of Common Prayer*

For a Difficult Situation

Lord,
help me to be faithful to you in this situation.
Help me to be your person,
a Christ-Bearer,
a Love Carrier,
in Jesus' name.

—Anon.

Looking Ahead

Dear Lord, I wonder as I get older and have more things go wrong with my body and my mind, what awaits me around the corner. I know I have to lay down this life before I can begin another, but I'm still a bit scared. I like it here. I love my family and friends. I enjoy the daily surprises. I even enjoy complaining! I want to live.

But I also believe, way down deep, that this life is but the first chapter in a much longer book. Turning the pages gets tougher as I near the end of this familiar story, but I realize that another chapter has to begin at some point; that I must let go; that death can be a friend rather than an enemy; that I must hang on to you, and have faith that you will carry me home to my true country, when the time comes.

What is around the corner still remains a mystery. What could happen later today or tonight or tomorrow is also uncertain. Therefore, please, dear Lord, help me relax and put my trust in you, my Savior and my Friend.

Whether I continue on in this life for awhile longer, or begin my new life sooner than I'd planned, it really makes no difference. For now I realize that nothing can or ever will separate me from you—neither pain nor fear nor time nor place nor life nor death. Literally nothing! I will stake my "life" on that.

Dear Lord, I place myself in your loving hands and ask you to ease my fears, touch my aches and pains, and hold me tight. Into your loving and eternal hands I commit myself—with new faith and in renewed hope.

There is a God. There is a new life that begins, not ends, with death. There is a tomorrow, and I'm convinced that I'll be in it!

Amen

—(The Rev.) Alanson B. Houghton

For the Loss of a Husband or Wife

Dear Lord Jesus Christ:
I accept the death of my beloved one,
and I give thanks
for the years we had together.
I entrust my dear one to your never-failing
care and love forever.

O Lord Jesus Christ:
Lead me in this new life of bereavement;
interpret to me its holy mysteries
and use me as your servant in it
to bless other lives.
Here am I;
Use me.

—(The Rev.) Charles Whiston
(Adapted)

Open-Handed Prayers

As I come to the end of this chapter, I find myself thinking of Francois Fenelon, a spiritual light in seventeenth century France. He wrote of prayer:

> Tell God all that is in your heart, as one unloads one's heart to a dear friend. Tell him your troubles that he may comfort you; tell him your joys that he may sober them; tell him your longings, that he may purify them; tell him your mislikings that he may help you conquer them; talk to him of your temptations, that he may shield you from them, show him all the wounds of your heart that he may heal them. . . . Blessed are they who attain to such familiar unreserved communion with God.

Following the same theme, pastor Francis Whiston advised a group of us on a weekend retreat to share our inmost thoughts with our Lord, holding them in his light and praying:

> These thoughts have come to me, O Christ,
> pass your holy judgment on them.

The Quaker author Thomas Kelly put it even more succinctly, as he prayed, "I open all before Thee."

Such open-handed prayers will be more than answered; they will change our lives.

Notes and
Index

Introduction

x: "O God . . . have you forgotten me?" Psalm 42:1, 9.

Chapter 1

Where Is God?

2: "deep waters," Psalm 69:2.

2: Esther de Waal, *Living with Contradiction* (Harrisburg: Morehouse Publishing, 1989, 1997), p. 129.

3: "My God . . . why have you forsaken me," Matthew 27:46.

4: F. L. Hosmer, "O Thou in All Thy Might So Far" (1876), *The Hymnal of the Protestant Episcopal Church in the United States of America* (New York: The Church Pension Fund, 1940), hymn 444.

5: "The Lord is my rock," 2 Samuel 22:2.

6: Max Lucado, *San Antonio Express News*, May 20, 1995.

6: "Father, into your hands," Luke 23:46.

7: "How long, O Lord," Psalm 13:1–3, 5, *New English Bible* (New York City: Oxford University Press, Cambridge University Press, 1961, 1970).

7: C. S. Lewis, *A Grief Observed* (London: Faber & Faber Limited, 1966), pp. 6–7, 59.

8: Thomas à Kempis, *The Imitation of Christ*, ed. and trans. Joseph N. Tylenda, S.J. (New York: Vintage Spiritual Classics, 1998), p. 68.

8: Thomas Merton, *Thoughts in Solitude* (New York: The Noonday Press, Farrar, Straus and Giroux, 1958), p. 83.

Chapter 2

WHAT ABOUT THOSE TIMES

WHEN PRAYERS ARE NOT ANSWERED?

10: Harry Emerson Fosdick, *The Meaning of Prayer* (New York: Association Press, 1945), pp. 114, 122.

11. Thomas R. Kelly, *A Testament of Devotion* (New York: Harper & Row Publishers, 1944), pp. 45, 47.

12: Frederick Buechner, *Wishful Thinking* (New York: Harper & Row Publishers, 1973), p. 71.

16: "stand far off," Psalm 10:1.

19: "for everything there is a season," Ecclesiastes 3:1 RSV.

19: Kay Lewis on her husband's illness, "My Theology of Prayer," *Theology in Scotland*, Vol. 1, no. 2 (Autumn 1994), pp. 75–80.

19: "I cry out," Psalm 22:2.

20: "save me—even from myself," Leslie F. Brandt, *Psalms/Now* (St. Louis: Concordia Publishing House, 1973), pp. 35–36.

20: "let this cup pass," Matthew 26:39 RSV.

22: A. J. Cronin, *The Green Years* (Boston: Little, Brown & Co., 1944), pp. 221, 311.

Chapter 3

HOW COULD A LOVING GOD LET THIS HAPPEN?

26: Peter Kreeft, *Making Sense out of Suffering* (Ann Arbor: Servant Books, 1986), p. 18.

29: "he went about doing good," Acts 10:38 RSV.

29: Henry Van Dyke, "Joyful, Joyful, We Adore Thee" (1907), *The Hymnal of the Protestant Episcopal Church in the United States of America* (New York: The Church Pension Fund, 1940).

30: Alfred, Lord Tennyson, "In Memoriam," 56, line 15, *The Norton Anthology of English Literature*, 4th Ed., vol. 2 (New York: W.W. Norton & Company, Inc., 1979), p. 1148.

31: Alan E. Lewis on the connection between human beings and the rest of the created order, *Theatre of the Gospel* (Edinburgh, Scotland: The Handsel Press Limited, 1984).

31: John MacArthur, *The MacArthur New Testament Commentary*, Romans 1–8 (Chicago: Moody Bible Institute, 1991), p. 455.

31: John Donne, "An Anatomy of the World, the First Anniversary," *The Norton Anthology of English Literature*, 4th ed., vol. 1 (New York: W.W. Norton & Company Inc., 1979), p. 1083.

32: Gerald R. Cragg, "Exposition on Romans," *The Interpreter's Bible*, vol. 9 (Acts & Romans), (Nashville: Abingdon Press, 1982), p. 519.

34: Peter Marshall, "Mr. Jones Meets the Master," *Sermons and Prayers of Peter Marshall* (New York: Fleming H. Revell Company, 1950), p. 71.

37: "did not understand," Job 42:3 NIV.

37: Everett Holland Jones, *Getting Life into Perspective* (San Antonio: Mini Mansions, 1983), p. 79.

37: Helen Smith Shoemaker, *The Exploding Mystery of Prayer* (New York: The Seabury Press, 1978), p. 2.

40: Leslie F. Brandt, *Psalms/Now* (St. Louis: Concordia Publishing House, 1973), p. 132.

Chapter 4

Ways to Come Close to God

43: Catherine de Hueck Doherty, *Poustinia* (Notre Dame: Ave Maria Press, 1975), p. 151.

43: "draw near to God," James 4:8 RSV.

43: C. S. Lewis, *Letters to Malcolm: Chiefly on Prayer* (New York: Harcourt Brace & Company, 1964), pp. 90–91.

43: "I see him when they smile," Jennifer Baird, "A Sunny Day in the Garden," *Guideposts Magazine,* June 1995, 3.

44: "the heavens declare," Psalm 19:1.

44: Jonathon Brown, *Puccini* (New York and London: Simon & Schuster, 1995), p. 15.

45: Charles Francis Whiston, *Pray* (Grand Rapids: William B. Eerdmans Publishing Co., 1972), p. 24.

46: St. Augustine, *The Confessions of St. Augustine,* trans. Edward B. Pusey, D.D. (New York: Collier Books, 1961), p. 131.

46: "I will both lay me down in peace," Psalm 4:8 KJV.

47. "fear not, little flock," Luke 12:32 RSV.

48: Thomas Merton, *The Seven Storey Mountain* (New York and London: Harcourt Brace & Company, 1948, 1976), p. 191.

49: Emil Brunner, *Truth as Encounter* (Philadelphia: Westminster Press, 1943, 1964), p. 108.

51: Everett Holland Jones, *Getting Life into Perspective* (San Antonio: Mini Mansions, 1983), p. 17.

52: Brother Lawrence, *The Practice of the Presence of God* (Old Tappan, New Jersey: Fleming H. Revell Company, 1958), p. 41.

53: Albert Schweitzer, *The Quest of the Historical Jesus* (New York: The Macmillan Company, 1968), p. 403.

54: "in him will I trust," Psalm 91:2 KJV.

55: John Greenleaf Whittier, "I Know Not What the Future Hath" (1867), *The Hymnal of the Protestant Episcopal Church in the United States of America* (New York: The Church Pension Fund, 1940), hymn 441.

56: Norman Vincent Peale, *The Power of Positive Thinking* (Englewood Cliffs: Prentice-Hall, Inc., 1956), p. 154.

57: *The Book of Common Prayer* (Proposed) according to the use of the Episcopal Church of the U.S.A., 1977, p. 831.

57: Thomas Merton, *The Seven Storey Mountain* (New York: Harcourt Brace & Company, 1948), p. 397.

58: Dag Hammarskjöld, *Markings* (New York: Alfred A. Knopf, Inc., 1964), p. 56.

58: Macrina Wiederkehr, *Seasons of Your Heart* (San Francisco: HarperSanFrancisco, 1991), pp. 7, 181.

Chapter 5

WHY I BELIEVE IN ETERNAL LIFE (AND THE DIFFERENCE THAT MAKES)

63: "my sheep hear," John 10:27 RSV.

63: "for God so loved," John 3:16.

63: "the gift of God," Romans 6:23 KJV.

64: "my peace I give," John 14:27.

67: "the earth is the Lord's," Psalm 24:1.

68: "no more death," Revelation 21:4.

69: Juliana of Norwich, *Revelations of Divine Love*, trans. M. L. del Mastro (New York: Image Books, 1977), pp. 131–132.

73: Thomas R. Kelly, *A Testament of Devotion* (New York: Harper & Row Publishers, 1941), p. 85.

74: John Cheever, "The Angel of the Bridge," *New Yorker*, 21 October 1961.

74: Frederick Buechner, *The Longing for Home* (San Francisco: HarperSanFrancisco, 1996), p. 110.

74: "eternity in the hearts," Ecclesiastes 3:11.

74: "you also will live," John 14:19.

75: Leslie F. Brandt, *Psalms/Now* (St. Louis: Concordia Publishing House, 1973), p. 141.

76: "I tell you the truth," John 16:20.

76: "a woman giving birth has pain," John 16:21–22

78: Psalm 139:1–3, 7–10, 23–24.

Chapter 6

Finding the Key to Answered Prayer

81: "Ask," Matthew 7:7 RSV.

83: Alan E. Lewis, lecture quoted in "My Theology of Prayer" by Kay Lewis in *Theology in Scotland*, vol. 1 no. 2 (Autumn 1994), pp. 75–80.

83: Anna B. Warner, "Being Perplexed I Say," *Daily Strength for Daily Needs*, by Mary W. Tileston (New York: G. P. Putnam's Sons, 1928), p. 249.

84: Eugene Kennedy, *This Man Bernardin* (Chicago: Loyola Press, 1996), p. 14.

85: Leslie D. Weatherhead, *When the Lamp Flickers* (New York, Nashville: Abingdon-Cokesbury Press, 1948), p. 150.

92: Eugene Kennedy, *This Man Bernardin* (Chicago: Loyola Press, 1996), p. 167.

93: "the love of God in Christ Jesus," Romans 8:38–39 RSV.

Chapter 7

A TREASURY OF PRAYERS THAT WILL ALWAYS BE ANSWERED

99: St. Francis of Assisi

100: Per-Olof Sjögren, *The Jesus Prayer* (Philadelphia: Fortress, 1975), pp. 84–85: copyright 1975 by the Society for Preserving Christian Knowledge.

101: Brother Lawrence, *The Practice of the Presence of God* (Old Tappan, New Jersey: Fleming H. Revell Company, 1958), p. 41.

101: Norman Vincent Peale, *The Power of Positive Thinking* (Englewood Cliffs: Prentice-Hall, Inc., 1956), p. 149.

102: "Use me today," prayer by Robert Ayres, Jr., "Use Me Lord," *Guideposts Magazine*, November 1979, 24.

102: "teach us to pray," Luke 11:1.

102: "Now is my heart troubled," John 12:27.

103: "I cannot do this unless you help me," Brother Lawrence, *The Practice of the Presence of God* (Old Tappan, New Jersey: Fleming H. Revell Company, 1958), p. 15.

103: "Help me, Lord," prayer by Robert Ayres, Jr., "Use Me Lord," *Guideposts Magazine*, November 1979, 19.

104: Leslie F. Brandt, *Psalms/Now* (St. Louis: Concordia Publishing House, 1973), p. 212.

105: "always giving thanks," Ephesians 5:20.

106: "bless the Lord," Psalm 103 KJV.

106: "all joy and peace," Romans 15:13 KJV

106: "I believe, help my unbelief," Mark 9:24 RSV

106: "into your hands I commit my spirit," Luke 23:46.

107: Grace Noll Crowell, "Prayer for Grown Sons," *The Wind-Swept Harp* (New York and London: Harper & Brothers Publishers, 1946), p. 32.

108: *The Book of Common Prayer* (Proposed) according to the use of the Episcopal Church of the U.S.A., 1977, p. 831.

109: (The Rev.) Alanson B. Houghton, "Benediction," ed. David A. Kalvelage (Milwaukee: The Living Church).

110: Charles Francis Whiston, *Pray* (Grand Rapids: William B. Eerdmans Publishing Company, 1972), p. 137.

111: Attributed to Francois de Salignac de la Mothe Fenelon (1651–1715), Archbishop of Cambrai.

111: Thomas R. Kelly, *A Testament of Devotion* (New York: Harper & Row Publishers, 1941), p. 61.

Index

of Prayers that Will Always Be Answered

Acknowledgments and Permissions

I would like to express my gratitude for the gift of working with Dan Penwell of Hendrickson Publishers; for the generous encouragement of the Rt. Rev. Jim Folts, Bishop of West Texas; the Rev. Mike Chalk; Robert Ayres, Jr.; and the Rev. Bill Collins, M.S.C.; and for the prayers, that have meant so much to me, of some very special people.

I also express my thanks to the following for their kind permission to include quotations in this book:

- Abingdon Press, *The Interpreter's Bible*, Volume 9 (Acts & Romans) copyright 1954 Pierce and Washabaugh in the United States of America, copyright renewal 1982 by Abingdon Press, and *When the Lamp Flickers* by Leslie D. Weatherhead, copyright 1948 by Pierce & Smith.
- Curtis Brown, Ltd., *The Seven Storey Mountain* by Thomas Merton. Copyright 1948 by Thomas Merton, Renewed. Reprinted by permission of Curtis Brown, Ltd. And also Curtis Brown, London, and Faber & Faber Ltd. for extracts from *A Grief Observed* by C. S . Lewis, copyright 1961, C. S. Lewis PTE Ltd., by permission of Curtis Brown, London. And also Curtis Brown, Ltd. and Farrar, Straus and Giroux, Inc. for excerpts from *Thoughts in Solitude* by Thomas Merton, copyright 1956, 1958, by the Abbey of Our Lady of Gethsemani.
- The Church Pension Fund of The Protestant Episcopal Church in the United States of America for use of the following hymns from *The Hymnal of the Protestant Episcopal Church in the United States of America*, 1940: Hymn #281, "Joyful, Joyful, We Adore Thee" by Henry Van Dyke; Hymn #444, "O Thou in All Thy Might So Far" by F. L. Hosmer; and Hymn #441, "I Know Not What the Future Hath" by J. G. Whittier.
- Concordia Publishing House, *Psalms/Now* by Leslie Brandt. Copyright 1973, Concordia Publishing House.
- William B. Eerdmans Publishing Co., *Pray* by Charles Francis Whiston, copyright 1972 by William B. Eerdmans Publishing Company.
- Guideposts Publishers for permission to adapt for use in the introduction of this book an incident I first wrote for them in *The Guideposts Home Bible Study Program*, copyright 1986 by Guideposts, Carmel, New York

10512, and prayers by Robert Ayres, Jr., taken from "Use Me, Lord," November 1979, *Guideposts Magazine*.

- Alfred A. Knopf, Inc., *Markings* by Dag Hammarskjöld, translation copyright l964 by Alfred A. Knopf, Inc.
- Harcourt Brace & Company, *The Seven Storey Mountain* by Thomas Merton, copyright 1948 by Harcourt Brace & Company and renewed 1976 by the Trustees of The Merton Legacy Trust, reprinted by permission of the publisher and also Harcourt Brace & Company and HarperCollins Publishers, Ltd. for excerpts from *Letters to Malcolm: Chiefly on Prayer* by C. S. Lewis, copyright 1964, 1963 by C. S. Lewis PTE Ltd. and renewed 1992, 1991 by Arthur Barfield, reprinted by permission of Harcourt Brace & Company.
- HarperCollins Publishers Inc., *A Testament of Devotion* by Thomas R. Kelly, copyright 1941 by Harper & Brothers; *Wishful Thinking* by Frederick Buechner, copyright 1973 by Frederick Buechner; *Seasons of Your Heart* by Macrina Wiederkehr, copyright 1991 by Macrina Wiederkehr; *The Longing for Home* by Frederick Buechner, copyright 1996 by Frederick Buechner; and "Prayer for Grown Sons," from *The Wind-Swept Harp* by Grace Noll Crowell, copyright 1946 by Harper & Brothers.
- Kay Lewis for permission to include some of the wisdom and insights from the writing and teaching of her late husband, Alan Lewis, as found in *Theatre of the Gospel* by Alan E. Lewis (Edinburgh, Scotland: The Handsel Press Limited, 1984) and in "My Theology of Prayer" by Kay Lewis in the periodical, *Theology in Scotland,* Vol. 1, No. 2, Autumn 1994, St. Mary's College, University of St. Andrews, Scotland.
- Liguori Trade, *Revelations of Divine Love* by Juliana of Norwich, published by Image Books, copyright 1977 by M. L. del Mastro.
- Little, Brown & Company, *The Green Years* by A. J. Cronin, copyright 1944 by A. J. Cronin, copyright renewed 1972 by A. J. Cronin.
- *The Living Church,* David A. Kalvelage, editor, for the prayer by Alanson B. Houghton.
- Loyola Press, *This Man Bernardin*, copyright 1996 John H. White. Chapter openers copyright l996 by Eugene Kennedy.
- The Moody Press, *The MacArthur New Testament Commentary: Romans 1–8* by John MacArthur. Copyright 1991, Moody Bible Institute of Chicago.
- Morehouse Publishing, *Living with Contradiction* by Esther de Waal, copyright 1989, 1997 by Esther de Waal.
- Random House, *The Imitation of Christ* by Thomas à Kempis, edited and translated by Joseph N. Tylenda, S.J., copyright 1984, 1998 by Joseph N. Tylenda, S.J.
- Fleming H. Revell, *The Practice of the Presence of God* by Brother Lawrence, eighth printing, 1974. Copyright 1958 by Fleming H. Revell Company.

- Servant Books, *Making Sense out of Suffering* by Peter Kreeft, copyright 1986 by Peter Kreeft.
- Simon & Schuster, *The Power of Positive Thinking* by Norman Vincent Peale. Copyright 1952 by Prentice Hall, Inc.; copyright renewed 1980 by Norman Vincent Peale.
- Simon & Schuster and Pavillion Books, Compact Companions: *Puccini* by Jonathon Brown, copyright 1995 by Pavillion Books, Ltd., text copyright 1995 by Jonathon Brown.
- Simon & Schuster and Rhena Schweitzer-Miller, *The Quest of the Historical Jesus* by Albert Schweitzer, translated by W. Montgomery (New York: Macmillan, 1968). Copyright 1968 by James Robinson.
- The Society for Promoting Christian Knowledge, *The Jesus Prayer* by Per Olof Sjögren, copyright 1975 by S.P.C.K.
- Westminster/John Knox Press, *Truth as Encounter* by Emil Brunner, copyright 1943 by Westminster Press and 1964 by W. L. Jenkins.